THE NEW
INTERCOURSES

an aphrodisiac cookbook

written and designed by
martha hopkins & **randall lockridge**
food photography by **ben fink**

TERRACE PUBLISHING

terrace publishing
800.372.2311
www.terracepartners.com
www.intercourses.com

International Standard Book Number
978-0-9653275-2-7
0-9653275-2-3

Library of Congress Control Number
2006908229

Printed in Canada
Published in the United States
by Terrace Publishing

Foreign Rights Available

Third Edition
1 2 3 4 5 6 7 8 9

The New InterCourses: an aphrodisiac cookbook

Originally published in the US, UK, and Australia in January 1997.
Revised and expanded edition published January 2007.
Copyright © 1997, 2007 by Terrace Publishing,
a partnership of Martha Hopkins and Randall Lockridge

Strawberries Drenched in Honeyed Cream adapted from *Basil* © 1993
by Janet Hazen. Used with permission of Chronicle Books LLC, San Francisco.
Visit ChronicleBooks.com. Adapted with permission of Janet Hazen.

Wild Mushroom Ragout excerpted from *Bittersweet* © 2003
by Alice Medrich. Used by permission of Artisan, a division of
Workman Publishing Co., Inc., New York. All rights reserved.

written and designed by: **Martha Hopkins and Randall Lockridge**
photography by: **Ben Fink**

hair and makeup (first edition): **Angela Angel**
food styling assistance (first edition): **Jeff Lehr**
food styling (ginger, seafood, and salmon): **Megan Fawn Schlow**
editorial assistance: **Lisa Asher, Carol Boker, and Barbara Elmore**
recipe testing and development: **Martin Barrera, Bénédicte Bosché,
Erica Bowie, Kristen Green, Ramona Ponce, and James Waller**

distributed to the book trade in the United States and Canada by
Independent Publishers Group
814 North Franklin St., Chicago, IL 60610
312.337.0747
www.ipgbook.com

distributed to the gift trade in the United States and Canada by
Sourcebooks, Inc.
1935 Brookdale Rd., Suite 139, Naperville, IL 60563
800.43.BRIGHT
www.sourcebooks.com

for turner

table of contents

Turn here for the heart of the matter – 19 chapters overflowing with more than 135 lip-smacking, finger-kissing recipes.

Even if you don't have a Whole Foods, Central Market, Wegmans, or Trader Joe's nearby, your neighborhood grocer most likely carries 95 percent of the ingredients listed in this book. For everything else, there's the internet. Take a look at some of our favorite purveyors.

If you like to cook, why stop with food? Expand your specialties to include tension-relaxing massage oils, melt-into-you bath oils, and clean-and-ready salt scrubs. Trade aphrodisiac dinners for backrubs or bath-time for two.

Overwhelmed by the romantic and/or erotic possibilities of all the recipes in InterCourses? Turn to this helpful guide to plan an aphrodisiac experience appropriate for any level of relationship, time of day, season of year, or even astrological sign of your partner.

thanks

To Ben Fink, for continuing to make beautiful art. • To all the models – Josh Bearden, Christine Clarke, Mollie Curlin, Bryan Greene, Dawn Grosser, Korbet Hayes, Kevin Jones, Natsuko Koizumi, Lisa Synder, Paul Riddick, and Sheila Thomas – who rose well above the call of duty. Our sincerest appreciation for your exceptionally hard work. • To all the testing couples – I'll not list names to protect the innocent (or guilty) – but we hope the food (and subsequent happenings) were as good for you as your contribution to *InterCourses* has been for us • To Walter Rose, for conceiving of the title. It has taken us far. • Thank you to Jeff Lehr, Angela Angel, and Carol Boker, our indispensable team for the first edition of *InterCourses*. And to the rest of the crew who made the original incarnation of the book a possibility: Patrick Pollei, Mary Margaret Ragland, Brad Meadows, Bob Smith, and all the folks at Mandarin Offset. • Thank you to the revised and expanded team for this new edition, a stellar bunch, to be sure: Lisa Asher, Martin Berrera, Bénédicte Bosché, Barbara Elmore, Kristen Green, Erica Martin, Ramona Ponce, Megan Schlow, and James Waller. We never would have met our deadline without your diligent, spot-on work. • To Denise Vivaldo, who first injected us with a hefty dose of confidence back in 1996 and has continued, steady, as a mentor, colleague, and friend since then. • To our friends Leigh Anne & Walter and Scott & Bryan. Thank you for nurturing us and our crazy ideas. • To Vlad and David. Thank God for Thanksgiving. • To Will & Mary K. and to Irene & Suzanne, our respective family members-turned-colleagues who supplied us with our creative genes and whose talent continues to make us beam with pride. • To Rogo, for being dad and best friend and honorary CFO and all-around Terrace lackey. You should ask for a raise. • To Pat and Carlene, moms extraordinaire. • To Dawn and Jeff, the loves of our lives, who put up with Terrace Publishing and all its eccentricities. Thank you.

preface

In January 1996, Randall and I were two and half years out of college. We had spent four years as close friends at Baylor University, living next door to each other in a vintage apartment named Terrace Gardens in Waco, Texas. After college, I moved back home to Memphis with a degree, a high GPA, and an assumption that life would be good. In fact, real life was a little more real than I had anticipated. I substitute taught, temped, and worked retail at Dillard's for two years. I finally got a "real" job, only to be fired after my first day. Randall eventually tired of my complaining and suggested we publish a book. With nothing left to lose, I said, "Sure!" • Twelve months later, with the help of our parents, friends, bosses, a brave banker, mild acquaintances, complete strangers, trusting models, and gaggle of excited recipe testers, we had written, designed, and published *InterCourses*. It appeared on store shelves in January 1997, just in time for Valentine's Day. • The month before it came out, Randall and I sat across from each other at Shoney's right off I-35 in Central Texas. Without showing each other our answers, we wrote down our best guess and biggest dream for the number of copies we would sell in the life of the book. We then took our scraps of paper and sealed them in an envelope marked "Open on December 15, 1997." • On my paper, I wrote 15,000 copies. Randall, ever the optimist, scribbled 25,000 copies. • Fast forward ten years, and we have now sold more than 200,000 copies to happy couples everywhere.

It seemed only right to celebrate this momentous occasion with a 10th anniversary edition, including updates from our original testing couples, fresh new recipes, and new testing couples (to spread the love). We altered recipes we'd wanted to tweak for years, add some new images, redesign the appendix, and update the resources page to include our now-favorite vendors. • We worked with Ben again, our fabulous photographer. We found more amateur models, one a visitor from Japan, the other a transplant from middle America to the Big Apple hoping to make it big. We checked in with many of the original models that we first accosted on the streets of Memphis with our Polaroid, excited to hear how their lives had transpired over the past 10 years. Randall married the asparagus girl, and my father performed the ceremony. We caught up with the original testing couples and found out that some had married, some had divorced, some had had babies, and most were in love. It was nice to hear from them all. • Working on the book felt euphoric and invigorating. It pumped happiness and life through our veins. We are grateful to all who have played a role in bringing both the original version and the new edition to fruition. • So here we have it, the revised, the expanded, *The New InterCourses*. It's like the old one, only better. Enjoy. Cook. Eat. Love. Live.

a p h r o

The word itself almost seems magical. On first glance, it conjures up images of Spanish fly, powdered rhino horn, and other strange, exotic ingredients meant to wield power over unsuspecting souls.

Throughout history, lovers have depended on love potions enhanced with charms of enchantment for those hearts stubborn to Cupid's arrow. Sometimes that meant a secret ingredient slipped into a goblet of wine. Other times, an elaborate concoction gulped down for stamina.

Historically, the qualifying factors for aphrodisiacs were relatively simple: The rarer an ingredient, the more likely it held aphrodisiacal qualities. Likewise, the more an ingredient resembled a sexual organ, the stronger its power over the libido.

Then intercontinental commerce and science entered the picture. With the emergence of a more global economy, tomatoes seemed not so rare, everybody had access to chocolate, and coffee became a staple of daily life. Science further de-mystified food, stripping age-old aphrodisiacs of their powerful qualities. Spanish fly? That simply aggravates the urogenital tract, creating a burning sensation that some associate with the heat of passion. Powdered rhino horn? It comes from a phallic-shaped, nutrient-packed tissue. Other than that, its power appears only psychological.

Coincidentally, many foods long considered aphrodisiacs are low in fat and high in vitamins and minerals. A diet heavy in these foods, then, yields a body healthy with the energy, blood-flow, and nutrients needed for a peak sexual experience.

d i s i a c

In providing explanations for improved sexual performance, science dispelled any connection between an ingredient's sexual appearance and its power over the human sexual experience, eliminating many a classic from the list of aphrodisiacs.

So what if an oyster resembles a slew of sexual organs? Science is science. Fact is fact. And everything has an explanation.

But explanation or no explanation, anyone who has ever fed a lover grapes knows that aphrodisiacs do exist. Anyone who has served an elaborate candlelit meal, painstakingly prepared with love, knows the potential power of food. We don't need scientific proof to know that aphrodisiacs exist; we need only experience them for ourselves to know that they are, in fact, a very potent force at our disposal.

And that's what InterCourses is for us: an introduction to the experience of aphrodisiacs. It's an experience for everyone — normal people, you and me — anyone who can cast aside fact and believe, if only for a moment, in the magic of food combined with a dash of ambiance or love. A sprinkling of sensuality or eroticism. A dollop of simplicity or grandiosity.

From the obligatory anniversary dinner to the unexpected glass of fresh-squeezed orange juice, the act of preparing food for another (or *with* another) speaks louder and clearer than most words. It says, with no exceptions, I love you. I want you. I care for you. You are worth the effort.

May InterCourses help you say what needs to be said.

bon appétit

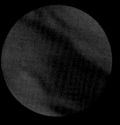

chocolate

With 200 wives to keep satisfied, the Aztec emperor Montezuma reportedly drank 50 cups of chile-spiked chocolate each day. Mayans traded cacao bean for a night at a the brothel (you'd be surprised at the options available for a mere handful of beans). The Marquise of Pompadour, a favored mistress of Louis XV, depended on chocolate to keep him aroused. Sixteenth-century church officials deemed it a sinful indulgence until Pope Pius V gave it a thumbs-up. And Casanova, the insatiable 18th-century lover, ate chocolate to sustain his stamina. • Richard Cadbury tapped into a veritable geyser when he packaged the first set of chocolates in a heart-shaped box back in 1861: worldwide sales of cacao beans topped 3.2 million tons in 2004 and, according to Mort Rosenblum's *Chocolate*, February 14th sales ring in at a hefty $1 billion. Most of that billion, one can assume, in heart-shaped boxes. Velvet preferred. • It takes only one little taste to understand what all the fuss is about: Its pure cocoa-butter base makes chocolate melt in the mouth, a pool of bitter and sweet and creamy on the tongue. It floods the body with so many antioxidants that blueberries and kale pale in comparison. With each snap of the couverture, it stimulates the body with caffeine, surges blood flow throughout the body with its flavonols, arouses us with cannabis-like fatty acids, and injects a dose of PEA and serotonin into our love-hungry veins.

chocolate-stuffed crescent rolls

easy twist on a french staple

2 ounces high-quality
dark chocolate

1 (4-count) package
crescent rolls

1 large egg yolk

1 tablespoon milk

2 tablespoons
turbinado sugar

I spent a summer in Paris. It was one of those rare occasions when the experience of something actually outmatches the dream, and memories of the event become a surreal vision in one's mind. While there, I became friends with a man named David. We would often go to a private club he belonged to and dance and laugh and talk all the night long, familiar – as if we had known each other for years. When the club would finally close at five the next morning, we would stroll to an all-night cafe for strong coffee and a chocolate croissant. This recipe is my quick-and-easy version of the classic French chocolate croissant and a jolt to my memory of our early mornings along the Champs Elysées. *[Update: I have no clue what happened to David, but I was fortunate to meet another Frenchman, with whom I have shared the last eight years of my life. We don't enjoy these crescent rolls together, because he always eats them all before I get a chance. More on him later.]*

YIELDS 4 ROLLS

Preheat the oven to 375 degrees. Cut the chocolate into 4 planks about ½ inch wide by 2½ inches long. Unfold the crescent roll dough. (For those foodies out there who cannot tolerate even the idea of a canned biscuit, feel free to use a bakery-fresh croissant. Make a slit in the side and slide your chocolate in. If your chocolate's good enough, it'll be superior to most any *pain au chocolate* you'll find in the States.) Place 1 piece of chocolate at the wide end of each piece of dough and roll up. Mix the egg yolk and milk in a small bowl. Brush on top of the rolls, sprinkle with the turbinado sugar, and bake 10 to 12 minutes, or until golden brown. Remove the croissants from the oven and loosen from the pan with a spatula. Let cool for 3 to 4 minutes before eating.

mexican hot chocolate

a classic central american favorite

The best way to experience Mexican hot chocolate is relaxing on a terrace overlooking the heart of Mexico. There, the twinkling lights of the nighttime city will dance for your eyes, and the warmth from the chocolate will embrace you. For a sensual home version, sit in your own back yard under the black sky of night and try a sip from the recipe below.

The most readily available brand of Mexican chocolate is Ibarra, which comes in a hexagonal package. If you can't find that, substitute bittersweet chocolate with a hefty pinch of cinnamon.

2 to 3 ounces Mexican
    chocolate
3   cups milk or water
    Cinnamon sticks for garnish

YIELDS 2 SERVINGS

Finely chop the chocolate by hand. It will shave off in grainy flakes. Place the chocolate in a blender. Set a saucepan over medium-high heat and add the milk. When the milk is warmed through and on the verge of boiling, pour the hot milk over the chocolate. Place the lid on the blender, cover with a towel for safety, and then pulse the mixture, removing the top to release steam if needed. Continue blending until the chocolate is completely melted and the milk is frothy. Pour into mugs and garnish with cinnamon sticks.

eve's just desserts

red foil

unfolding
to reveal
shapes
beneath
over
longing
to kiss
thin
lying, lips
dark Belgium

conquest
demanding
return

Barry McCann, Colorado Springs, CO

chocolate-almond truffles

sweet chocolate dessert candies

Confectioners around the world have long known the exaggerated power of chocolate combined with nuts. And anyone who has ever tasted gianduja – an ecstasy of hazelnut essence and creamy chocolate – or secretly craves Hershey's Kisses with the little sliver of almond has an idea of where the following recipe can take you. The flavor won't compete with something like one of Michael Recchiuti's unstoppable confections, but it will still taste fabulous. And that's the great thing about homemade aphrodisiacs – it really is the thought that counts.

YIELDS 8 TO 12 TRUFFLES

Chop the almonds in a food processor until coarsely ground. Remove half of the almonds and set aside for coating the truffles. Add the chocolate to the food processor and process until finely ground. Add the almond pie filling and almond extract; process until the mixture begins to come together. With the motor running, add the coffee and liqueur. Process until the mixture thins slightly and becomes smoother. Refrigerate 1 hour to harden slightly.

To roll the truffles, chill your hands by rubbing them with an ice cube or dunking in ice water periodically, and then patting dry. Roll the chocolate mixture into ¾-inch balls, and then roll in the ground almonds. Place on a waxed-paper-lined tray or plate and refrigerate until ready to serve.

½ cup whole almonds or hazelnuts, toasted

4 ounces high-quality bittersweet chocolate

1 tablespoon almond pie filling

⅛ teaspoon almond extract

1 tablespoon strong hot coffee

1 tablespoon hazelnut liqueur

black russian cake

a serious chocolate cake

for the cake:

Butter for greasing

1   cup vegetable oil

4   large eggs

3/4   cup strong coffee

1/2   cup crème de cacao

1/4   cup Kahlúa

1   package dark-chocolate
    cake mix

1   (3½-ounce) package instant
    chocolate pudding

for the topping:

1½ cup confectioners'
    sugar, sifted

3   tablespoons strong coffee

3   tablespoons Kahlúa

3   tablespoons crème de cacao

A few years back, my roommate had a crush on one of her classmates. As they worked long, hard hours on a project together, she wooed him to the best of her ability, but he did not seem to be taking the bait. As is typical of many men, he knew that he liked her . . . but did she like him?

Then she made him this cake. (Well, actually, *I* made the cake because she had to work the late shift.) Anyway, it's now four years later, and they have just purchased their first dog together. It's a pug named Kato, and if he were allowed to eat chocolate, he'd like the cake too. *[Update: Said couple has now gotten married, courtesy of my father, the retired Baptist minister. The wedding was an intimate, beautiful affair, and the bride giggled her way down the aisle, as she is wont to do. They have added an additional pug to the fray named Ling Ling. I suspect Ling will be a might jealous when their new baby arrives. He (it's a boy!) is due just in time for the release of this book on Valentine's Day 2007.]*

YIELDS 12 SERVINGS

Preheat the oven to 350 degrees and thoroughly grease a 10-inch Bundt pan or a tin of miniature Bundts.

For the cake, combine the oil, eggs, coffee, crème de cacao, and Kahlúa in a large bowl. Mix well with a wooden spoon. Add the cake mix and pudding mix, and stir until just combined. Pour into the Bundt pan until three-fourths full. (Save any remaining batter for cupcakes or simply eat on the spot.) Bake 45 to 50 minutes, or until a skewer inserted comes out clean of batter. (For miniature Bundts, reduce the baking time to 20 to 30 minutes.) Invert the cake onto a serving plate and punch holes throughout the cake with a skewer or ice pick.

While the cake is baking, prepare the topping. Be sure to sift the confectioners' sugar well, or the glaze is sure to be lumpy. Combine the confectioners' sugar, coffee, Kahlúa, and crème de cacao until the sugar dissolves. Spoon over the warm cake, reserving several tablespoons to drizzle onto cut slices. Serve warm or at room temperature.

toasted nutella
and banana sandwiches

seduction, elvis-style

Think of this treat as a late-night re-energizer. No sweet sandwich could be simpler or yummier. For best results, use a bakery-fresh Pullman loaf of white bread (though Pepperidge Farm's Farmhouse Hearty White also performs admirably).

Our test-kitchen results sound a bit staid compared to Scott's experience. "Nutella is a gift straight from the GODS! Add bananas, and it's pure heaven! What a great, messy dessert to share with your partner – the Nutella gets everywhere, but it's easily licked off. Yee Haw!" *Scott, a cowboy in disguise, together with Hugh for 14 years, Portland, OR*

2 slices good white bread

2 heaping tablespoons Nutella

1 large ripe banana

Y I E L D S   2   S E R V I N G S

Toast the bread slices. Spread each with 1 heaping tablespoon Nutella. Cut the banana in half crosswise, then cut each half lengthwise into 4 or 5 thin slices. Lay the slices atop the sandwiches and serve. For a variation, spread the sandwiches with a mixture of Nutella and creamy peanut butter (1 heaping tablespoon of each, stirred until thoroughly combined).

indoor s'mores for grown-ups

gooey. sticky. messy. yummy.

8   *graham crackers, halved*

1   *(3½-ounce) bar dark chocolate, finely chopped*

4 to 8 Jet Puffs marshmallows

According to legend, the s'more (a contraction of "some more" – as in "you can't eat just one") was invented by some enterprising Girl Scouts in the 1920s, and it has since become an emblematic food of American childhood. Well, there's no reason we adults – with our slightly more sophisticated tastes – can't have our own s'mores (and eat them too). Graham crackers slathered with a good, dark bittersweet chocolate are the right choices for our aged and jaded demographic. But when it comes to the marshmallows, stick to good old Jet Puffs; "decorator" marshmallows just don't toast as well. As for the chocolate, we fixed the age-old s'more issue of the chocolate not melting sufficiently in time for that first gooey bite by pre-melting the bar.

YIELDS 2 TO 4 SERVINGS

Lay the graham cracker halves on a work surface. Place the chocolate in a microwave-safe bowl and heat for 1 minute at 50 percent power. Stir and microwave for another 30 seconds at 50 percent power. Stir again. If the chocolate hasn't completely melted, continue microwaving, but be sure not to overheat. (If you want to melt your chocolate ahead of time, you now have the opportunity to use that mini crockpot that's been collecting dust. Simply place the chopped chocolate in the crockpot, set on low, and stir occasionally until melted. The crockpot will keep the chocolate at a beautiful, melty consistency until you're ready to use. If it seems too hot, unplug and let the insulated bowl keep the chocolate warm.)

Brush the chocolate onto each half of the graham crackers with a pastry brush or spread with a knife. Now, toast the marshmallows. The method is completely up to you. We prefer skewering 1 to 2 marshmallows on the narrow end of a chopstick or metal skewer, holding it very near (but not in) the flame of a stovetop burner, and gradually twirling the marshmallow until the entire surface is lightly browned and the interior is hot and gooey. (If you're feeling adventurous and especially romantic, you and your partner might try toasting the marshmallows above a grouping of three or four votive candles — but please don't set your house on fire!) As soon as it's toasted — and while it's still hot — place each marshmallow atop the melted chocolate and cover it with another graham cracker, pressing down on the sandwich to ensure that the squished marshmallow oozes into the chocolate. Eat immediately. And don't forget to share.

wild mushroom ragout

dark chocolate adds a layer of depth

Greg and Eden have been together nine months in the appropriately Eden-like setting of San Luis Obispo. Together they tested Alice Medrich's sublime combination of earthy mushrooms and rich, dark chocolate from one of my favorite books of hers, *Bittersweet*. In it, Alice offers insight into the chemistry of cooking with the plethora of high-cacao-percentage chocolates available today. With so many artisan chocolates flooding the market, those flavorless, waxy bars of your youth will soon seem a distant memory.

"We sat across from each other, dripping in sweat (it was one of the hottest days of the year), looking deeply into each other's eyes, licking chocolate/red wine reduction sauce off of each other's fingers, with Israel Kamakawiwo'ole strumming lightly and soulfully away on his ukulele in the background," says Greg.

For Eden, who had come home from a tedious day at work both hungry and tired, "All it took was a little sautéing and a bit of simmering, and there we were with a delicious meal. The complex interaction of complementary flavors that first hit my mouth was a bit surprising and overwhelming, and yet, the more I ate, the more I wanted. (A bit like our relationship, frankly.) Finally I decided to abandon all cutlery and give into the sloppy, slurpy mess that became of my fingers and face. To this moment, I cannot tell if it was the ragout I wanted more of or the licking that resulted from the mess I made of it."

YIELDS 4 TO 6 SERVINGS

1 pound mixed mushrooms, such as portobellos, chanterelles, shiitake, cèpes, and cremini

2 tablespoons olive oil, divided

2 cloves garlic, finely minced

2/3 cup dry red wine, such as Rioja or Merlot

1 to 2 pinches freshly grated nutmeg, ground cardamom, white pepper, and ground cloves

1/4 teaspoon salt

1/4 cup water

1 tablespoon finely chopped unsweetened chocolate

Keeping the different mushrooms separate, rinse them briefly and pat dry. Slice 1/4 inch thick, discarding the stems if they seem tough. Set a large skillet over medium-high heat and add about a teaspoon of olive oil. Add one type of mushroom and sauté, stirring frequently until browned, 2 to 3 minutes. Scrape them into a bowl and set aside. Repeat with each mushroom type, scraping them into the same bowl. If you are not using a nonstick pan, you may want to dissolve the browned bits from the pan in between each batch and scrape the juices and bits into the bowl.

Set the pan over medium-low heat and add 1 more tablespoon of olive oil and the garlic; sauté until soft but not browned. Return the mushrooms and any accumulated juices to the pan. Add the wine, spices, and salt, and simmer for 2 to 3 minutes.

Add 1/4 cup of water, cover, and simmer for 6 to 10 minutes to cook the mushrooms and release their juices into the sauce. Uncover and cook until the sauce is reduced and slightly syrupy. Stir in the chocolate until it melts and smoothes the sauce. Taste and correct the seasonings, if necessary. Serve over polenta, toast points, or anything plain that absorbs the rich flavors of the sauce.

chocolate torte dressed in berries

oh baby

1 cup toasted almonds, finely chopped

6 tablespoons unsweetened cocoa powder

2/3 cup unsalted butter, softened

1 cup sugar

1/4 cup brown sugar

4 large eggs

1 teaspoon vanilla

1/2 cup chopped fresh strawberries, plus more berries for garnish

1/2 cup strawberry preserves

1/4 cup heavy cream

6 ounces high-quality dark chocolate, finely chopped

Fresh mint sprigs for garnish (optional)

"I knew that my husband had a business dinner that night. But I told him before he left that morning to save room for dessert when he came home. The anticipation was enough to drive me crazy. He got home around eight o'clock. I left a note on the entrance hall table where he always stops and sets down his briefcase. The note instructed him to go into the dining room, where I left a second note – and a blindfold – on his plate. The note instructed him to put on the blindfold. He did, and then I walked into the room and said in a stern voice, 'Are you ready for your just desserts?' He said, 'Yes,' a tinge of fearful excitement in his voice. 'Okay, take off your blindfold,' I said. He did, and the look on his face was priceless. There I was, naked except for some strategically placed whipped cream and holding the moist chocolate cake dressed in berries. I asked, 'You did leave room for dessert, didn't you?' He didn't answer, but I guess he did because he ate two desserts that night. *Danielle and Rick, married 12 years, Tulsa, OK*

YIELDS 6 TO 8 SERVINGS

Preheat the oven to 350 degrees. Combine the almonds and cocoa powder in a small bowl. In a large mixing bowl, cream the butter and sugars with an electric mixture until fluffy. Beat in the eggs and the vanilla. Fold in the almond mixture and then the fresh strawberries.

Thoroughly grease the bottom and sides of an 8- or 9-inch springform pan. Spoon the batter into the pan and bake for 45 minutes, or until a toothpick inserted in the center comes out clean of chocolate batter.

Cool the cake completely. Remove from the pan, and place on a serving plate or cake stand. (The cake is extremely fragile and moist, so you may prefer to leave it on the base of the springform pan.) Spread the top of the cake with the strawberry preserves.

Bring the cream just to a boil in a small saucepan. Remove from the heat and add the chocolate. Stir until smooth. Pour the chocolate over the top of the cake, and let drizzle down the sides. Decorate the melted chocolate with strawberry slices around the edge and a whole strawberry or sprig of mint in the center of the cake. Refrigerate if not serving immediately.

chocolate-hazelnut madeleines

best warm from the oven

"The golden foamy butter turns to caramel and laces through the delectable deep dark chocolate."
Mary and Neil, married 16 years with 3 beautiful little girls, Hamilton, MA

My French friend Bénédicte, who has been making these cookies since her childhood, swears that you must make a minimum of two versions of madeleines at a time. Otherwise, the single version would feel lonely. We paired these decadent madeleines with some more lady-like Honey Lemon-Thyme ones (see page 88). Serve with hot tea or coffee, in real china, like civilized folk. What you do after you consume them is your own business.

YIELDS 30 MADELEINES OR 48 MINI-MUFFINS

Butter and flour enough madeleine tins for about 30 cookies or 48 mini-muffin tins, being careful to get into all the little creases where the madeleines are most likely to stick. Use a butter spray if you prefer. Set a large saucepan over medium-high heat. Add the 13 tablespoons of butter and let cook until it foams and begins to turn golden brown and smell nutty, about 3 to 5 minutes. Remove immediately from the heat and pour into a small bowl to stop the cooking.

Place the chocolate in a microwave-safe bowl and microwave — uncovered — at 50 percent power for 1 minute at a time, stirring in between each heating. (Be careful, as chocolate can scorch easily, ruining your madeleines.) Remove the chocolate from the microwave when almost melted, and continue stirring to melt any remaining bits.

Sift the sugar and the flour together in a medium mixing bowl. Add the ground hazelnuts, stirring to distribute. Place the egg whites in a large mixing bowl and beat with an electric mixer until frothy. Add the sugar mixture and fold together with the egg whites. Pour in the browned butter, honey, and melted chocolate. Beat to incorporate.

Pour the batter into the buttered and floured molds, filling them almost to the top. Cover and refrigerate for at least 1 hour to let the batter set. Preheat the oven to 375 degrees. Bake for 12 to 15 minutes, or until cooked through and springy to the touch. Remove from the oven, lightly bang the pan to loosen the madeleines, and invert to unmold. Cool slightly on a wire rack before serving, or cool completely before storing. They will keep for 2 to 3 days in an airtight container.

13 tablespoons (1½ sticks plus 1 tablespoon) unsalted butter, plus more for greasing

All-purpose flour for dusting

5 ounces high-quality bittersweet chocolate, finely chopped

1⅔ cup confectioners' sugar

½ cup plus 1 tablespoon all-purpose flour

½ cup finely ground hazelnuts or ½ cup high-quality cocoa powder

6 large egg whites

1 tablespoon honey

a s p a r a g u s

These stalks first received their aphrodisiac status from the Doctrine of Signatures. Also known as the Law of Similarities, this theory says that if one thing looks like or is reminiscent of another, then it will improve or aid that which it looks like. So if food looks sexual, then the Doctrine of Signatures says it is meant to improve or aid sex. • And indeed, asparagus is a beautiful (albeit slender) phallic symbol. Sometimes embarrassingly and obviously so. Lascivious, in fact, as Richard Burton has said. It's finger food extraordinaire, easy to prepare, and positively dripping with sensuality—and butter, if you're lucky. • French lovers of yesteryear dined on three courses of the white and green spears on the night before their wedding. Today we know that asparagus is packed with potassium, phosphorous, calcium, and vitamin E. It offers the love-hungry extra energy, a well-working urinary tract and kidneys, and a natural dose of the "sex vitamin" necessary for increased hormone production. One course of asparagus should be enough for the desired results, but the French understand well the ways of love. Follow their example if you wish.

sautéed asparagus with a toasty topping

asparagus adds elegance to any plate

1   bunch asparagus, trimmed

1½ tablespoons olive oil

  Salt and freshly ground
  black pepper to taste

for the breadcrumb topping:

1   teaspoon olive oil

¼ cup fresh breadcrumbs

¼ cup chopped walnuts
  or almonds

¼ teaspoon garlic powder

¼ cup chopped fresh chervil

1   tablespoon chopped
  fresh parsley

  Salt and freshly ground
  black pepper to taste

It's hard to screw up fresh asparagus. Yes, it can be done, but not if you hold fast to the philosophy of less is more. If you look at the asparagus and think, "Hey, that spear's beginning to look a little limp," then make haste and get that asparagus off the fire! This holds true for all preparations of this alluring vegetable, my favorite of which is sautéing. Unlike steaming and blanching, which both have their place in the world of asparagus, sautéing and roasting add a brownness, a crispness lacking in other preparations. If the weather's right, grilling adds yet another dimension of flavor. But for the rest of the year, I recommend sautéing. If you're short on time, feel free to skip the toasted topping altogether. But if you're one of those people who makes her macaroni and cheese in an extra-large casserole dish just to increase the surface area of crispy toppings, then you won't want to miss this one.

YIELDS 4 SERVINGS

Set a large sauté pan or grill pan over high heat. Rinse the asparagus well, but don't pat dry. Drizzle with the olive oil and toss to coat. Place the asparagus into the hot pan and season with salt and pepper. Toss several times with tongs, and then cover and reduce the heat to medium or medium-high. Shake the pan or toss the asparagus occasionally for even cooking. If the spears are beginning to burn, add ½ cup of water to the pan. (Alternatively, grill over a hot fire for 4 to 6 minutes.)

To prepare the topping, set a small skillet over medium-high heat and add the oil. Add the remaining ingredients, swirling in the pan and toasting lightly until fragrant and slightly crunchy.

When the asparagus is just tender enough to eat and slightly charred on the outside, it's ready to serve. Remove to a warmed serving platter and top with the toasted breadcrumb mixture.

pasta with asparagus, chicken, and gorgonzola

bold combination of flavors

As is the case with artichokes, many people do not quite know how to approach asparagus. Try this: Trim the asparagus by gently bending each stalk near the base to break off the tough, woody ends. Peel the skin off the bottom 2 inches of any thicker or older stalks using a peeler or paring knife. Your asparagus is now ready for cooking.

YIELDS 2 TO 3 SERVINGS

Bring a large pot of salted water to a boil. Cut the asparagus into 1½-inch lengths. Blanch the asparagus for 2 to 3 minutes, or until just crisp-tender. Remove the asparagus from the water, and add the linguine to the boiling water. Cook until al dente. Reserve ½ cup of the pasta water, and drain the noodles.

Melt the butter in a large skillet set over medium-high heat. Add the chicken strips, and season with salt and pepper. As the chicken begins to brown, add the shallot. Continue cooking just until the shallot begins to soften. Stir in the cream, scraping the bottom of the pan to release any browned bits. Stir in the red pepper flakes. Add the Gorgonzola cheese, stirring to melt. Taste and add more salt and pepper if needed.

Add the tarragon, cooked asparagus, and linguine and toss to coat evenly with the sauce. If the sauce seems too thick, add some of the reserved pasta water and cook until reduced to the desired consistency. Place on a warmed platter and garnish with Parmesan and fresh tarragon.

½ pound asparagus, trimmed

½ pound linguine

1 tablespoon unsalted butter

1 chicken breast, cut into thin strips

Salt and freshly ground pepper to taste

1 shallot, finely chopped

½ cup heavy cream

Red pepper flakes to taste

2 ounces Gorgonzola cheese, crumbled

1 tablespoon fresh tarragon leaves, plus several whole sprigs for garnish

¼ cup freshly grated Parmesan cheese

chicken, asparagus, and black bean enchiladas

what tex-mex could be

3/4 pound asparagus, trimmed (12 to 18 stalks)

4 slices bacon

1/2 pound boneless, skinless chicken thighs, cut into thin strips

2 cloves garlic, crushed

1 1/2 cups salsa, divided, plus more for garnish

1 (15-ounce) can black beans, undrained

1 small green bell pepper, chopped

1/2 teaspoon ground cumin

1/4 teaspoon chile powder

Salt and freshly ground black pepper to taste

1/4 cup sliced green onions

Oil for greasing

6 fresh corn tortillas

3/4 cup shredded Monterey Jack cheese

1/2 cup light cream

Chopped tomatoes for garnish

Sour cream for garnish

As this recipe calls for blanched asparagus, you might want to seize this opportunity to make your own version of the asparagus skirt shown at the beginning of the chapter. We promise it's fun. Just trim your asparagus and blanch as usual. Using a needle and substantial thread or lightweight fishing line, thread the asparagus onto the string. Tie around hips and continue preparation of the meal. When it's time for the asparagus to go home to their tortillas, simply pull the spears off with a firm tug, wrap in a tortilla, and bake according to the directions. *[Update: Randall tied the original skirt onto the "asparagus girl," as she so fondly came to be known to us during the photo session. After a few seconds of shooting, the skirt fell apart, the fishing wire cutting through the tender spears. Randall quickly salvaged what he could of the skirt and tied it back around her hips, knotting it for security. Nine years later, he married the model, tying the knot officially this time.]*

YIELDS 2 TO 3 SERVINGS

Bring a large pot of salted water to a boil. Blanch the asparagus until bright green, but still crisp. Rinse under cold water to stop the cooking. Blot dry. Cook the bacon in a skillet over medium heat until crisp. Remove from skillet, drain on paper towels, and crumble. Pour off all but 1 tablespoon of the bacon drippings.

Sauté the chicken and garlic in the drippings until the chicken is just cooked. Stir in 1/4 cup salsa, the beans, bell pepper, cumin, and chile powder. Season with salt and pepper. Simmer for 7 or 8 minutes, or until thickened, stirring occasionally. Stir in the green onions and reserved bacon.

Preheat the oven to 350 degrees and grease a 9 x 9-inch baking dish. To assemble the enchiladas, spoon the bean mixture down the center of each tortilla. Add 2 to 3 asparagus stalks and top with the cheese, reserving 1/4 cup for garnish. Roll up each tortilla and place, seam-side down, in the dish. (The enchiladas can be prepared to this point a day in advance and refrigerated until ready to bake.)

Combine the remaining salsa with the cream and pour over the top. Bake for 15 minutes (or 30 to 45 minutes if the enchiladas have been refrigerated), or until warmed through. Sprinkle on the remaining cheese. Bake 5 minutes longer, or until the cheese is melted and bubbly. Serve with chopped tomatoes, sour cream, and additional salsa, if desired.

"The meal seemed to energize my lower chakras, stirring their depths to rise up with impelling, creative force . . ."

Jeff, in response to the *pasta with asparagus, chicken, and gorgonzola* (page 25) and his lower-chakras-stirring partner, Isabelle, married 9 years, Memphis, TN

steamed asparagus with coco's homemade mayonnaise

a hands-on experience

1 bundle of white or green asparagus, or a combination of each

1 large egg, separated

1 tablespoon Dijon mustard

⅛ teaspoon salt

⅛ teaspoon freshly ground black pepper

1 tablespoon white wine vinegar, or other vinegar of your choice

½ cup extra-virgin olive oil

"You will think to yourself, 'But it's just a little egg.' You will think to yourself, 'I've made it through life this far without an electric mixer.' You will try to whip that egg white with a whisk. Oh, yes. You will try. And you will fail. Look, making mayonnaise is a serious undertaking. It takes time. It takes care. It takes patience. You're not getting any younger, you know. Go ahead. Make the commitment. Buy an electric mixer.

"Or, you know, if you really just want to watch each other sweat, go ahead and use the whisk. I guess it won't matter at that point. It'll still be tangy and slippery and good, even if it hasn't come together quite perfectly. And let's be frank: you're going to be feeding each other gooey, dripping stalks of asparagus. Are you really going to notice if your mayonnaise isn't quite emulsified?" *Sophie, together with Erik for 6 years, New York, NY*

YIELDS 4 SERVINGS

Fit a large stockpot with a steamer basket and tight-fitting lid and fill with enough water to come just below the steamer basket. Set over high heat and bring to a boil. Prepare an ice bath in a large bowl. Trim the asparagus, snapping or cutting off the bottom third of each stalk where it naturally breaks. If using white asparagus, peel the outer skin with a vegetable peeler, starting just below the head and peeling to the base.

Thick stalks of asparagus need more cooking time than thin stalks, white stalks more time than green. So, depending on your combination of colors and thickness, add the asparagus to the steamer basket that will take longest to cook and season with salt. Add the thinner spears toward the end of cooking. Cover tightly and let steam until tender enough to eat, but still slightly crisp, about 8 to 10 minutes for thicker stalks, 4 to 5 minutes for thinner. Plunge the asparagus in the ice bath to stop the cooking, and pat dry with a towel.

While the asparagus is steaming, whip the egg whites in a mixing bowl with an electric mixer until they form soft peaks. In another bowl, combine the mustard, salt, pepper, vinegar, and egg yolk. (You can use the same electric mixer as you did for whipping the whites — just be sure to whip the whites first, not second, or they won't peak.) With the mixer running, drizzle in the olive oil and mix until (continued) completely emulsified. Taste for seasonings and add more if needed. Add the whipped egg whites into the mayonnaise, and fold in until all the whites are incorporated. It will be a frothy, fluffy mixture with the yolk paled by the addition of the whites. Refrigerate until ready to serve with the steamed asparagus. To serve, arrange the cooked asparagus in a clear glass, standing upright with the spears pointing upward. Spoon the mayonnaise into a serving bowl. Dip the spears into the mayo and enjoy. Or, as Sophie recommends, "Grab the asparagus with your bare fingers, and go for it. If you drizzle the sauce on top and then use a fork, it will ruin the whole goofy, filthy, phallic-y-ness of it." Use any leftover mayonnaise for a sandwich spread or veggie dip.

asparagus-prosciutto rolls

easy and delicious

These rolls are good finger food. Sure, the vinaigrette might dribble on your chin and the asparagus might slip out to find itself a new home and the cream cheese might put a white dab on your rosy cheek. As I was saying, these rolls are good finger food.

YIELDS 2 TO 3 SERVINGS

Bring a large pot of salted water to a boil over high heat. Prepare a large bowl of ice water. Add the asparagus to the boiling water and cook for 3 to 4 minutes, or until bright green and just tender. Remove the cooked spears and dunk in the ice water to stop the cooking, and then drain and pat dry.

For the vinaigrette, combine the vinegar, mustard, honey, garlic, shallot, salt, and pepper in a mixing bowl with a whisk. Pour in the olive oil and whisk well until emulsified.

To assemble the rolls, set a slice of prosciutto on a clean surface. Spread ½ tablespoon of the goat cheese on the prosciutto with an offset spatula. Set 1 thick spear or 2 thin spears of asparagus on the cheese near the bottom of the prosciutto slice, and roll up the asparagus in the prosciutto. Drizzle the rolls with the vinaigrette, garnish with the chives, and serve immediately.

6   stalks thick asparagus or 12 stalks thin, trimmed

1   tablespoon white wine vinegar

1   tablespoon Dijon mustard

½   teaspoon honey

1   clove of garlic, thinly sliced

1   small shallot, minced

Salt and freshly ground black pepper to taste

3   tablespoons extra-virgin olive oil

3   thin slices prosciutto, cut in half crosswise

3   tablespoons goat cheese or cream cheese, divided

1   tablespoon minced fresh chives for garnish

chilled asparagus and ginger soup

buttermilk adds some zip

3 tablespoons extra-virgin olive oil, divided

1 leek, white part only, thinly sliced

1/4 to 1/2-inch piece of fresh ginger, grated

Half a bundle of asparagus, about 15 stalks, trimmed

1 cup buttermilk, plus more as needed, or 1 cup milk plus 1/2 cup sour cream

1 cup vegetable stock, plus more as needed

Salt and freshly ground black pepper to taste

1/4 dried guajillo chile pepper, minced, or 1/2 dried serrano chile pepper, minced

Paprika for garnish (optional)

"As a gentlemen never talks about the glorious moments that follow an aphrodisiac recipe such as this, may I just suggest to future cooks that spoon-feeding this soup to your partner will yield unexpectedly wonderful reactions. Blind-folded tastings help reveal even more of the flavors and effect of the ginger."

BDH, married 1 year to SH, Montreal, Canada

YIELDS 2 TO 3 SERVINGS

Set a medium sauté pan over medium-low heat and add 1 tablespoon of the olive oil. Sauté the leek and ginger until soft and yellow, taking care not to let them brown, about 6 to 8 minutes. Remove from the heat.

Fill a large saucepan with enough water to come about an inch up the sides and fit with a steamer basket. Set over high heat and bring to a boil. Cut the trimmed asparagus into thirds and reserve the tips. Place the rest of the pieces in the steamer and cover with a tight-fitting lid. Steam only until crisp and bright green, no longer than 3 to 4 minutes at the most. Remove the strainer and place the cooked asparagus in the pan with the leeks. Steam the reserved tips in the same pot for one minute, until crisp and bright green. Remove from the strainer and reserve for garnish.

Combine the leek-asparagus mixture, the buttermilk, stock, salt, pepper, and the remaining 2 tablespoons of the olive oil in a blender. Cover and blend on medium-high until all of the asparagus chunks have been processed. Carefully uncover, adjust the salt and pepper to taste, and add more stock or buttermilk to reach the desired consistency. Add the dried pepper; pulse three to five times.

Serve immediately or chill in refrigerator for an hour. Just before serving, pour into two soup plates and drizzle with a spoonful of buttermilk, if desired. Garnish with the reserved asparagus tips and extra dried pepper, if you're feeling extra spicy. Sprinkle with paprika for color, if desired.

savory french toast with asparagus and gruyère

a hot, baked sandwich for grown-ups

"Who'da thunk it? How seriously aged Gruyère leads ineluctably to senseless shagging? 'Tiz one of life's quotidian mysteries, proof positive that our world is full of amazing, erotic surprises." *Bendrix, waxing eloquent on Savory French Toast, together with Sarah for 16 years, Fort Worth, TX*

YIELDS 2 TO 4 SERVINGS

Preheat the oven to 400 degrees. Combine the milk, eggs, salt, and pepper in a mixing bowl and whisk thoroughly. Dip each slice of bread into the egg mixture, being sure to coat thoroughly, and place in a medium casserole dish. Pour any remaining egg mixture over the bread and let sit for 15 to 30 minutes to soak.

While the bread is soaking, bring a medium pot of salted water to a boil. Prepare a bowl with ice water. Blanch the asparagus slivers for 2 to 3 minutes, or until bright green and still crisp. Drain and then plunge into the ice water to stop the cooking. Drain again and pat dry.

Line a heavy jelly-roll pan with parchment paper. Butter the parchment to keep the toast from sticking. Place half the bread slices on the paper. Sprinkle each slice with the sage and thyme. Place slices of the cheese on top of the herbs, and arrange the blanched asparagus on top of the cheese. Season with salt and pepper to taste. Spread a thin layer of Dijon on one side of the remaining pieces of bread. Place the slices, Dijon-side down, on top of the asparagus, and slightly press down to make the sandwiches stay together.

Bake until browned on the outside and warmed and custardy on the inside, about 25 minutes.

3/4 cup whole milk or half-and-half

3 large eggs

Salt and freshly ground black pepper to taste

6 or 8 (1-inch-thick) slices stale ciabatta or sourdough bread, enough to make 4 small sandwiches or 3 larger ones, or 2 stale croissants, sliced in half

6 to 8 stalks asparagus, trimmed and sliced thinly on the diagonal

Butter for greasing

1 tablespoon chiffonade of fresh sage

1 teaspoon fresh thyme leaves

3 ounces high-quality Gruyère or Swiss cheese, thinly sliced

1 to 2 tablespoons Dijon mustard

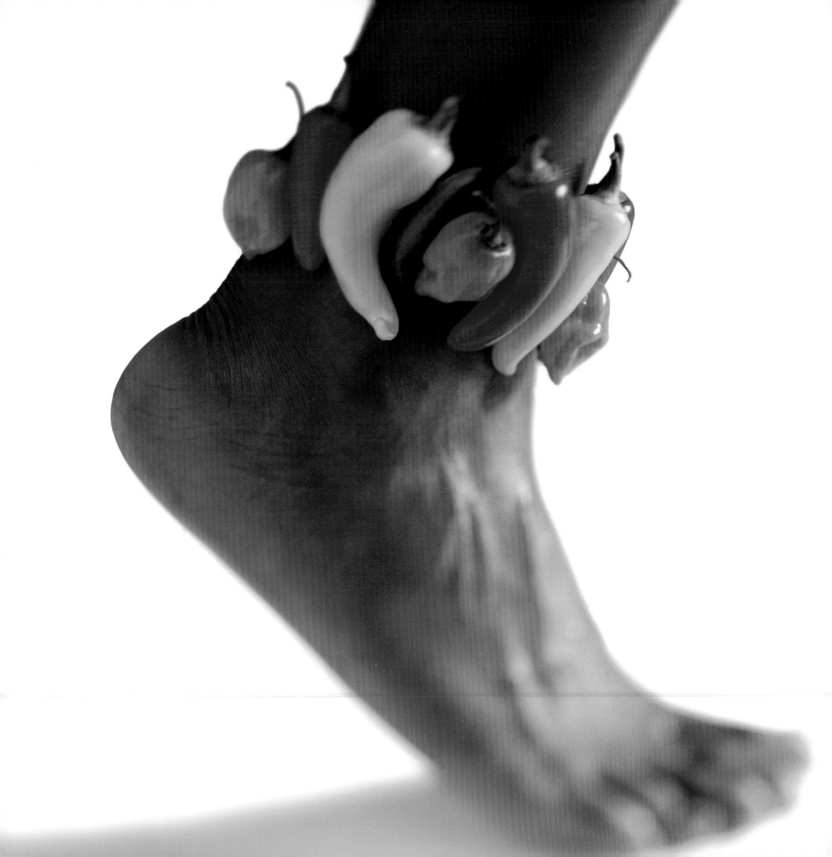

c h i l e s

Long believed to house a complete arsenal of aphrodisiac powers, chile peppers can fire up an otherwise bland dish, spicing up an entire evening in the process. With more than 200 varieties worldwide, chiles seem to have as many options for heating things up as clever lovers do. There's the firecracker hot of the tiny red-orange pequín that explodes in the mouth with the first bite. The heated sweet of the wrinkled pepperoncini. The delayed fireball of the dark-brown chilaca that lurks behind other flavors until it's ready to take charge. The gently pleasing spice of the slender, green Anaheim. • Dr. John Harvey Kellogg, inventor of Corn Flakes and founder of the Kellogg cereal company, knew what he was talking about when he advised nymphomaniacs to stay away from peppers. Eating chiles gets the blood rushing, the heart pumping, the face flushing, and the pores sweating — all reactions strangely familiar to what one can experience with anything from a good-night kiss at the front door to a heated quickie during lunch hour.

thai chicken
with peanut sauce

fiery taste, entertaining to roll

for the marinade:

1   tablespoon soy sauce

2   cloves garlic, minced

2   teaspoons sugar

1   tablespoon peanut oil

    Zest and juice of ½ lime
    (about 1 tablespoon juice)

    Freshly ground black pepper
    to taste

2   boneless, skinless chicken
    breast halves

for the dipping sauce:

2   teaspoons vegetable oil

2   cloves garlic, minced

    Szechuan hot chile
    bean paste, to taste

¼   cup chicken broth

2   tablespoons unsweetened
    coconut milk

1½ tablespoons creamy
    peanut butter

1   teaspoon soy sauce

    Pinch of sugar

1½ tablespoons chopped
    peanuts

for garnish:

    Large green or red leaf
    lettuce leaves, washed well
    and dried

½   cup fresh mint leaves

½   cup fresh cilantro leaves

2   tablespoons sesame seeds,
    toasted

One afternoon, I could not live another minute without some hot panang curry, so I headed to my favorite establishment. Sitting alone, I entertained myself by watching the table across from me: two Thai teenagers, both about 16. They sat across from each other, both leaning back, smoking, and trying to look cool in that way that only 16-year-olds can. Underneath the table, I could see some subtle foot action beginning to unfold – nothing obvious, but enough for a keen voyeur like me to detect. When the food arrived, he picked up a roll, dipped it in the peanut sauce, and fed her. She bit it and smiled. They ditched the cool act and fed each other the entire meal, amidst giggles and "inadvertent" touches. And I could see from the look in their eyes that they were in love.

YIELDS 2 TO 3 SERVINGS

To prepare the marinade, combine the soy sauce, garlic, sugar, peanut oil, lime, and pepper in a large, resealable plastic bag. Rinse the chicken and pat dry. Pound slightly until both breasts are of even thickness throughout. Add the breasts to the marinade. Chill in the refrigerator for 1 hour or longer, flipping occasionally to redistribute the marinade.

While the chicken is marinating, prepare the dipping sauce. In a small saucepan set over medium heat, add the vegetable oil and sauté the garlic for 1 to 2 minutes, being careful not to burn. Stir in the chile paste and continue to cook for 30 seconds. Add the broth, coconut milk, peanut butter, soy sauce, and sugar; whisk to blend. Bring to a boil, reduce heat, and simmer for 2 minutes to thicken, stirring frequently. If using the sauce immediately, stir in the peanuts. (The sauce can be made up to two days in advance and stored in the refrigerator. When ready to serve, warm slightly in a small saucepan to thin and add the chopped peanuts.)

Prepare a medium-hot grill or preheat the broiler. Drain the chicken from the marinade, and discard the marinade. Grill the chicken for 3 to 4 minutes per side, or place under the broiler, turning once. Grill just until cooked through, being careful not to overcook. Remove from the grill and slice thinly on the diagonal. (continued)

While the chicken is grilling, assemble a platter with the large lettuce leaves, mint, cilantro, and small bowls with the toasted sesame seeds and dipping sauce. Serve the chicken alongside the platter of condiments. To assemble the rolls, place a few slices of chicken on a large lettuce leaf. Garnish with the mint, cilantro, and sesame seeds. Roll up the leaf like a burrito or eggroll, dip in the peanut sauce, and enjoy with some plum wine or Sapporo beer.

salsa oaxaqueño
authentic taste of southern mexico

Oaxaca captured my heart the minute my train chugged into the station. I went there for a summer and lived with a family in a colonia called Indeco Xoxo. My friends and I would often go into town for an evening of salsa – dancing, that is. We would don our floral skirts, gossamer blouses embroidered in electric colors, and huaraches all bought earlier that week at the big market. And off we would go for an evening of *bailar*, breaking all sorts of mores in this old-school Mexican town. The spicy flavors of this recipe capture a bit of how we felt on those Oaxacan nights, dancing on the cobblestones outside our favorite salsa clubs.

YIELDS ABOUT 2 CUPS

2   tomatoes, finely diced or 1 can diced tomatoes

½   red onion, finely diced

¼   cup tomato juice

1   clove garlic, crushed

¼   cup chopped cilantro

   Juice of 2 limes

   Salt and freshly ground black pepper to taste

1   small chipotle pepper in adobo, seeded and minced

Combine the tomatoes, onion, tomato juice, garlic, cilantro, and lime juice in a bowl. Season with salt and pepper. Stir in half the chipotle pepper. Taste and add more, if desired.

The salsa can be made in a blender or food processor as well, but the result will be thinner. Chill, covered, for up to 2 days. Serve with fresh corn tortillas.

come-to-jamaica wings

rum adds a fun dimension to the bite

¼ cup freshly squeezed
   lime juice (4 to 5 limes)

2 tablespoons dark rum

2 tablespoons honey

1 to 2 jalapeño peppers,
   thinly sliced

2 tablespoons soy sauce

2 tablespoons cider vinegar

1 teaspoon allspice

1 clove garlic, minced

¼ teaspoon cinnamon

¼ teaspoon finely grated
   fresh ginger

¼ teaspoon habanero sauce
   or other hot sauce

½ teaspoon dried thyme

2 generous pinches each
   salt and freshly ground
   black pepper

¼ cup grapeseed or
   vegetable oil

2 pounds large chicken wings,
   tips discarded and
   wings rinsed

"First, she said, hot then sweet. Pepper. Honey. Then, she whispered, sweet and then hot. Her hands slid then clutched. They honeyed then peppered. I kept thinking what a wicked, wicked angel."

Walter, on how much he loves his spicy wings and his spicier Jane, together 5 months, Boston, MA

YIELDS 2 TO 3 SERVINGS

Combine all the ingredients except for the wings in a large plastic storage container. Shake well to mix. Separate the wings at the joint to make 2 sections per wing. Add to the marinade and toss well to coat. Refrigerate for 24 hours.

Prepare a medium fire. Drain the wings well. Grill for 4 to 5 minutes per side over indirect heat, or until cooked through and slightly charred. Alternatively, broil for 15 to 20 minutes, turning once, or until cooked through.

"This was the first meal I ever made for my new boyfriend, so I was very excited to see how the meal (and the evening) would go. The shrimp was a very aromatic dish — the lemon grass, garlic, ginger — they all heightened my senses throughout the preparation. We ate the meal by candlelight, enjoying both the food and the company. After dinner, we ran down to the store for some more wine, only to find his apartment robbed when we returned! All aphrodisiac power permanently drained from us (or so I thought), we had to deal with cops, locksmiths, and insurance claims until 2:00 a.m. But when we finally fell into bed, all the stress of the evening behind us, our thoughts once again turned to the shrimp and its hot spicy fiery sizzling heat. And I felt hotter for him than I'd ever felt for anyone before."

Kim, on preparing *spicy gingered shrimp* (page 104)
for Taylor, first at-home dinner, Fairfax, VA

indian-spiced lamb gyro

an intensely flavored experience

- 1 teaspoon freshly squeezed lemon juice
- 1 teaspoon balsamic vinegar
- ½ cup plain yogurt
- 1 teaspoon minced fresh ginger
- ½ teaspoon minced garlic
- ½ teaspoon ground coriander
- ¼ teaspoon ground cumin
- ¼ teaspoon cayenne pepper
- ¼ teaspoon turmeric
- ½ teaspoon salt, or more to taste
-   Freshly ground black pepper
- 1 pound lamb steaks from the leg or loin, 1 inch thick
- 2 whole pita rounds or 4 pita pockets
- 1 tablespoon olive oil
- 3 leaves red or green leaf lettuce, shredded
- ½ cup peeled, thinly sliced cucumber rounds
-   Mint mayonnaise (recipe follows)

I met a boy in Paris who played table tennis. Competed, even, and won. I first met him and his sandy hair and dreamy eyes in front of Notre Dame. But it is my last night out with him, some weeks later, that relates to the gyro and my own personal happiness.

We were wandering about the streets of Paris, trying to decide where to go, but not really deciding much of anything. We happened by a gyro stand; he bought a gyro for himself and stole an orange for me from the fruit stand next door. We wandered a bit farther until we came upon an old church with wide front steps. There we sat, he with his gyro on one step, me with my orange on the step below. Between bites, he murmured something that I couldn't quite catch. I turned my head to look back over my shoulder and ask him what he'd said. But instead of repeating his comment, he caught my head in the crook of his elbow and kissed me, sweet and light, the citrus taste of my lips mixing with the spicy coating on his. I felt that unassuming kiss down to my toes. *[Update: Philippe became a high school chemistry teacher at a rough high school in Paris. Fed up with the derelict teenagers, he quit his job, moved to the town of Chantilly, and became a kindergarten teacher. He wrote to me on September 12, 2001, to make sure I was okay. We corresponded once or twice that week, and I hadn't heard from him since. When I wrote to find out an update on his life for the book, crossing my fingers that the six-year-old email address was still active, he responded with a long note and four pictures of himself from recent trips. How do I say this without offending my boyfriend? Well, I can't. Here's the truth: I found his letter so charming and his pictures so dadgum hot that I felt like a giddy school girl for three days straight – complete with butterflies, silly grin, and all.]*

YIELDS 2 TO 4 SERVINGS

Place the lemon juice, vinegar, yogurt, ginger, garlic, coriander, cumin, cayenne, turmeric, salt, and pepper in a medium mixing bowl. Stir to combine. Add the lamb to the marinade, coating well. Cover and refrigerate at least 4 hours.

While the lamb is marinating, prepare the mint mayonnaise (on the next page) and prepare a hot grill. Grill the lamb 4 to 5 minutes per side, or until medium-rare. Remove from the grill, tent lightly with aluminum foil, and let rest 5 minutes. (continued)

While the lamb is resting, brush the pita rounds with olive oil and heat on the grill, in the oven, or in a sauté pan on the stovetop until warmed through and beginning to crisp.

To assemble the sandwiches, thinly slice the lamb against the grain on the diagonal, sprinkle with additional salt if needed, and serve with shredded lettuce, cucumber rounds, and a thick schmear of mint mayonnaise on the grilled pita. Fold and eat.

mint mayonnaise

great on the daily turkey sandwich, too

YIELDS ABOUT 3/4 CUP

Combine the mint leaves, cilantro, sprouts, jalapeño, and onion in a food processor or blender. Process until finely chopped. Add the vinegar and mayonnaise, and pulse just until blended. Chill, covered, until ready to use.

½ cup loosely packed fresh mint leaves

½ cup loosely packed fresh cilantro leaves

¼ cup alfalfa sprouts

½ jalapeño pepper, chopped

1½ tablespoons chopped onion

1 teaspoon cider vinegar

¼ cup mayonnaise or yogurt

pom's refreshing thai beef salad

bright tastes for a light lunch

Pom runs the front of the house for Bangkok Royal, one of my favorite restaurants in Waco and some of the best Thai in Texas. My boyfriend, Jeff, has fallen head-over-heels for their Panang, my co-author, Randall, gets weak in the knees from their Pad See Euw, and I spent a full year in submission to the Shrimp in Coconut Cream with Frizzled Basil. Of late, though, my loyalties have shifted to this zippy, puckeringly sour, yet simultaneously sweet salad. It does a dance on the field greens and bathes the steak with refreshing flavor. Think cold shower on a hot morning. This recipe comes courtesy of Pom's mother, the cook.

YIELDS 2 LARGE OR 4 SMALL SERVINGS

for the dressing:

- 2 teaspoons fish sauce
- 4 tablespoons freshly squeezed lime juice
- 2 tablespoons sugar
- 1 teaspoon ground Thai chile
- 2 tablespoons sweet chile paste (Pom uses the Pantainorasingh brand)
- ¼ cup thinly sliced garlic

for the salad:

- ½ pound flank or skirt steak
- 1 tablespoon peanut oil
- Salt and freshly ground black pepper to taste
- 1 bag organic lettuces, preferably mâche or field greens
- ¼ cup chopped fresh mint leaves
- ¼ cup chopped fresh cilantro leaves
- ¼ cup sliced green onion
- ¼ cup seeded and diced cucumber
- ¼ seeded and diced tomato
- ½ cup thinly sliced red onion
- ¼ cup chopped roasted peanuts

To prepare the dressing, combine all the ingredients, stirring well to dissolve the sugar.

Remove the flank steak from the refrigerator while preparing the dressing and let come to room temperature. Prep all the ingredients for the salad before dressing the lettuce. Set a grill pan over high heat or prepare a hot grill. Drizzle the peanut oil on each side of the steak. Massage into the meat. Generously season with salt and pepper. When the pan is hot, cook the meat for 2 to 3 minutes per side for medium-rare, or until the desired degree of doneness. Remove the meat to a plate and let rest 5 minutes. Thinly slice on the bias, going against the grain.

Place the lettuce in a large mixing bowl. Drizzle with several tablespoons of the dressing and toss lightly with your hands to coat the leaves. Be careful not to over-dress, as this dressing is zippy. Add more dressing if needed.

Place the mint, cilantro, green onion, cucumber, tomato, and onion in a small bowl and drizzle with dressing. Stir gently to coat.

To serve, make a bed of dressed greens and arrange the grilled flank steak on top. Spoon the herb mixture over the steak, and sprinkle with roasted peanuts. Serve immediately, or the lettuce will wilt.

chipotle mac

southwestern overtones on a classic

The first meal I ever made was cheese toast in my Easy Bake Oven. Once I mastered that, I moved on to what is still one of my most favorite dishes ever: macaroni and cheese. There are a myriad of variations on the classic, most involving a béchamel sauce and a bit of effort, which is not always conducive to aphrodisiac experiences.

On one of my trips to France to visit Jeff's family, his mother served us a noodle gratin. We gobbled it up. When I found out how simple the dish was to prepare, it became an instant addition to my quick-fix dinner repertoire. I probably make it more than I should, but I love the way it brings out the – how shall I say this? – Frenchness in him.

In this version, I've added some adobo sauce to the crème fraîche. You may not notice the heat at first, but it will send you a little kick and warm your throat toward the end of the bite.

Angela has found great success with the Chipotle Mac as well. "Besides being ready when you are, this recipe is absolutely delicious and has just the right amount of spice to heat things up . . . in more ways than one. My husband and I wanted to lick the bowl at the end of the meal, among other things." *Angela and John, acquaintances for 16 years, best friends for 7, and married for 5, Charleston, SC*

- 8 ounces penne pasta
- 1 tablespoon adobo sauce*, or more if desired
- 1 (8-ounce) carton crème fraîche

  Salt and freshly ground black pepper
- ½ cup freshly grated Parmesan cheese

YIELDS 4 SERVINGS

Bring a large pot of salted water to a boil over high heat. Preheat the broiler. Add the penne and cook according to package directions until al dente. While the pasta is cooking, add the adobo sauce to the container of crème fraîche and stir together. Taste and add more adobo, if desired. Drain the noodles and pour into a small casserole dish. Season with salt and pepper. Add the crème fraîche mixture and stir until all the noodles are well coated. Sprinkle with the Parmesan cheese and place under the broiler for 2 to 3 minutes, or until the Parmesan has turned golden brown and is beginning to crisp. Serve immediately.

* From a small can of chipotles in adobo, found in the Mexican-food section of most supermarkets

cozy vegetable korma

a mild, creamy curry

¼ cup raw cashews, plus ¼ cup toasted and chopped for garnish

1½ teaspoons coriander seeds

1 medium clove garlic, crushed and minced

1 teaspoon finely grated fresh ginger

½ teaspoon ground cumin

¼ teaspoon ground turmeric

Pinch of ground cinnamon or cloves (optional)

3 tablespoons corn oil

4 dried hot red chiles, left whole

1 bay leaf

1 medium onion, diced

1 medium sweet potato, peeled and cut into 1-inch chunks

1 large parsnip, peeled and cut into 1-inch chunks

1 chayote, peeled, seeded, and cut into 1-inch chunks

1½ cups basmati rice

2 tablespoons olive oil

½ small head of cauliflower, trimmed and broken into bite-size florets

½ cup peas, fresh or frozen

¼ cup plain yogurt (preferably thick, Mediterranean style)

⅓ cup half-and-half

Salt to taste

"Korma is a cozy dish, and we are a cozy couple. Danny and I piled white basmati rice into two deep soup bowls, spooned the korma over the rice, and headed to the couch. Lounging side-by-side on the couch under a shared blanket, holding warm bowls in our laps, we groaned "yum" to each other after each bite. The lasting smells of curry and freshly steamed rice hung in the air through the night, but the aromas of ginger, garlic, and coriander clung to our clothes and hair until morning." *Anneliese and Danny, Atlanta, GA*

Sam and Megan, married two years in San Diego, CA, had equally delicious results. "The smell of the spices filled our apartment, which we affectionately call the love nest. Sam was in the office/guest room while I was cooking, but the aroma led him to the kitchen, where he began kissing my neck while I stirred the vegetables. It was a good thing the recipe called for some simmering time because we were definitely simmering. By the time we were ready to eat dinner, we were already satisfied, but the flavorful dance of spices in our mouths just made us hungry for more."

You'll find that the dried whole chiles liven up the mild curry flavor of this korma, which includes the South American squash known as chayote among its medley of vegetables. (Chayotes – green, smooth-skinned, and nearly spherical – can be found in many supermarkets.) Serve the korma as the main dish for dinner, and enjoy any leftovers for lunch the next day. It's one of those dishes that – though excellent when first made – improves after a day in the fridge.

YIELDS 4 TO 6 SERVINGS

In a small bowl, cover the ¼ cup raw cashews with ⅓ cup boiling water and let stand for 20 minutes. Using a mortar and pestle, grind the coriander seeds to a powder, then add the garlic, ginger, cumin, turmeric, and cinnamon (if desired) to the mortar and grind to a paste.

Heat the oil over medium heat in a large, heavy-bottomed saucepan. Add the chiles and bay leaf and cook for 30 seconds. Add the spice paste, onion, and ¼ cup water and stir. Cook until the onion is translucent, about 7 minutes. Add the sweet potato, parsnip, chayote, and ½ cup water. Cover and simmer for 15 minutes. (continued)

While the vegetables are cooking, prepare the basmati. Set a large saucepan over medium to medium-high heat. Add the olive oil, and then stir in the rice, coating evenly with the oil. Cook, stirring frequently, until the rice begins to turn white and smells pleasantly nutty. Be careful not to burn. Add 2½ cups water or stock, increase the heat to high, and bring to a boil. When it reaches a boil, cover with tight-fitting lid and turn to the lowest heat possible. Continue cooking until the water is absorbed and the rice is tender, about 15 minutes.

Place the cashews and their soaking water in a blender and purée. Add the cashew purée, cauliflower, peas, yogurt, and half-and-half to the saucepan and stir to combine. Cover again and turn the heat to the lowest possible setting. Simmer until all the vegetables are tender, about 15 minutes. Season with salt to taste. (Note: This dish may be kept on the stove, on very low heat and an occasional stirring, for several hours without harm.) Serve with the basmati rice and garnish with the toasted cashew pieces.

c o f f e e

Nothing beats a cup of joe. It's everywhere, all the time. It probably became an aphrodisiac by default. We drink it in the morning to wake up. We drink it after dinner to close the meal. We have coffee in bed, on the couch, at the table. We mix it with cream or sugar, or skim and fake sugar, or honey, no cream please. We ice it down when we're hot. We froth it up when we're cool. We drink regular, decaffeinated, imported, gourmet, flavored, blended. We use instant granules for speed, a French press for the richest taste, and a programmable drip for a Monday morning alarm. Whether in fine china or a mug, a demitasse or tall Italian glass, coffee is an aphrodisiac we use daily. • Who knows why anyone first believed the coffee bean enhanced love? Maybe it's the dark, rich color of a freshly brewed pot. Or its pleasingly bitter scent wafting through the air. Or the jolt of caffeine it pumps through our blood. Or its alkaloids that help maintain sexual performance and delay the inevitable for a few sweet, luscious seconds. Or maybe it's just because when you offer someone coffee, you are welcoming them to sit down and stay awhile. And friendliness is *always* attractive.

grilled lamb chops with coffee rub

penetrating spices come to life on the grill

1 teaspoon kosher salt

¾ teaspoon finely milled dark-roasted coffee beans

¾ teaspoon freshly ground black pepper

¾ teaspoon garlic powder

¾ teaspoon sweet paprika

¾ teaspoon dried rosemary

¾ teaspoon dried thyme

2 lamb shoulder chops, ¾ to 1 inch thick

When used as a spice, coffee has a curious effect: It awakens and harmonizes the other flavorings, even as it contributes its own nutty and even slightly wine-like taste to the mix. Longtime (passionate) cook Elise concurs, "From the moment I read the ingredients in the recipe, my head was filled with visions of Dave's seasoned lips, and my mouth began to water. Fortunately, the marinating time gives you ample time to do practically anything your heart desires." *Elise and Dave, together 5 years and betting on more, West Fairlee, VT*

This rub, which also incorporates another aphrodisiac botanical (rosemary), is custom-tailored for grilled lamb. Fatty, meaty shoulder chops work best — and they're less expensive than other lamb chops.

YIELDS 2 SERVINGS

Thoroughly combine the salt, coffee, herbs, and spices in a small bowl and rub the mixture on both sides of the chops. Cover with plastic wrap and let stand at room temperature for 1 to 2 hours.

Prepare a hot grill. For medium-rare chops, grill for about 5 minutes per side, turning once.

mascarpone clouds

coffee and brandy in fluffy suspension

¼ cup heavy whipping cream, chilled

½ cup mascarpone cheese, softened

2 tablespoons freshly ground espresso coffee beans

2 to 3 tablespoons sugar

4 teaspoons brandy

2 tablespoons slivered almonds, toasted

2 tablespoons chocolate-covered espresso beans

"It was a highly unusual dish with spectacular after-effects. There's enough Baylor University left in me to be reticent about the particulars, but let's just say that the earth shook and the heavens cried out. Sorry, but that's all the detail you get." *Ben and Julia, together 6 years, St. Paul, MN*

YIELDS 2 SERVINGS

Whip the heavy cream to soft peaks in a mixing bowl with an electric mixer. In a separate bowl, but with the same mixer, beat the mascarpone cheese to soften. Add the ground coffee beans, sugar, and brandy, and continue mixing until well combined. Fold the whipped cream into the mascarpone mixture. Cover and chill for at least 2 hours.

To serve, place several dollops in dessert glasses and sprinkle with toasted almonds and chocolate-covered espresso beans.

ice cream and espresso affair

hot & cold, yin & yang

"The espresso was instantly cooled by the ice cream, which provided a creamy delivery on the palate. It was a bit messy to eat with a spoon; doing so left dribbles down my chin, but Jeff didn't miss a drop. He's an espresso man anyway, and the creaminess of this dish just about sent him over the edge. I served his with vanilla ice cream and mine with chocolate. Thank goodness for Blue Bell Great Divide. I'm sure it's saved many a marriage with its no-compromise solution to the endless chocolate vs. vanilla debate."
Lisa and Jeff, together 8 years, Bedford, TX

1 pint high-quality vanilla, chocolate, or coffee-flavored ice cream

2 shots freshly brewed espresso

YIELDS 2 SERVINGS

Divide the ice cream between 2 serving bowls or large cups. Set in the freezer to harden until ready to serve. Brew the espresso (or make a run to the corner coffee house). Pour the hot espresso over the frozen ice cream and enjoy.

café atole

chocolate + coffee with a hint of heat

As Aaron tells it, "I was in New York for the weekend and went by one of my favorite galleries to see what they were showing. A girl walked over to me and introduced herself as Dominique. Considering how shy I am with strangers, it's a good thing she made the first move. We started talking, went to an auction, continued talking, went window shopping, kept on talking, and decided to go down the street for some coffee. We sank down into one of the cafe's big, fluffy sofas and, over a cup of hot mocha chocolate, I found out she was a millionaire many times over. I've always considered that I got lucky that night – just on a different level than usual."

3 cups milk

¼ cup finely chopped, high-quality dark chocolate

2 tablespoons sugar

Pinch of cayenne pepper, or more to taste

1 cup strong coffee

3 tablespoons fresh masa

YIELDS 2 SERVINGS

Combine the milk, chocolate, sugar, and cayenne in a medium saucepan set over medium-high heat. Bring to a simmer, whisking constantly until the chocolate is melted. Stir in the coffee and the masa, whisking vigorously until well combined. Taste and add more cayenne, if desired. Let thicken slightly and then serve.

"the buttery-brown liquid

our porch.

reminded me of his perfect

our swing.

skin as I sat sandy-eyed

his bathrobe, my cup.

and blissful on our porch."

rondalyn, on coffee and her michael, together 7 months, atlanta, ga

frozen coffee-almond dessert

enticingly cold and smooth

"Testing this recipe with Patrick brought back a flood of memories of the days we first met. I was out one hot July night walking home with a friend, and we passed an outdoor coffee shop called the Pop Stop. I saw a guy sitting at a table alone, his feet up on a drain. Our eyes met, and as I passed, I waited a few seconds, turned — he did the same — and we gave each other a huge smile.

"I placed an ad in the 'glances' section the next week (my first classified, I might add): 'Pop Stop 7/6. You — sitting outside at a table alone. Me — walking by with a friend. We exchanged smiles; how about phone numbers?' Two days later, he called. He was so excited, sincere, even a little innocent — something you don't find these days. We met for ice cream, talked for hours, and had our first kiss. It was wonderful.

"As I wrote him a bit later, 'Here's to coffee shops, ice cream, and classifieds.'" *Patrick and Tracy, in love for 2 months, Washington, DC [Update: Patrick and Tracy broke up 8 months later, but their story was not over. After the heartache subsided, Tracy actually set Patrick up with his friend, Nick. Fireworks ensued, and Patrick and Nick have now been together for nine years. Tracy wasn't left to cry crocodile tears of loneliness either. He and his partner, Frank, have been together for eight years. The best part: "We consider them our best friends," Patrick says. "They even hosted the rehearsal dinner for our wedding at their house, in celebration of our marriage in November 2003."]*

3 almond-macaroon cookies

3 chocolate graham crackers

1½ tablespoons rum

1½ tablespoons Kahlúa

1 pint coffee ice cream, softened

¼ cup grated or finely chopped high-quality bittersweet chocolate

⅓ to ½ cup heavy whipping cream, chilled

½ tablespoon superfine sugar (optional)

¼ teaspoon vanilla extract

½ (4-ounce) package sliced almonds, toasted

YIELDS 4 TO 6 SERVINGS

Crumble the macaroons together with the graham crackers in a small bowl. Stir in the rum and Kahlúa. Line the bottom of an 8 x 8-inch freezer-safe casserole dish with the macaroon mixture and pat down evenly. Spread with the ice cream, and then sprinkle with the chocolate shavings, pressing down slightly so they stick in the ice cream. Freeze at least 2 hours to let the ice cream set up.

When ready to serve, whip the cream with the sugar (if desired) and the vanilla until soft peaks form. Spread on top of the chocolate, and sprinkle with the toasted almonds. Cut into squares, carefully remove with a flat spatula, and serve immediately.

chocolate-dipped meringue with espresso cream

meringue melts like cotton candy on the tongue

for the meringue:

½ cup confectioners' sugar

¼ cup granulated sugar

2 large egg whites, room temperature

Pinch of salt

for the chocolate:

3½ ounces high-quality dark chocolate, preferably 70% cacao or higher, finely chopped

for the espresso cream:

1 cup (½ pint) heavy whipping cream, chilled

3 tablespoons light brown sugar

1 teaspoon vanilla extract

1 tablespoon instant espresso

"This is a formula for sensuality as much as it is a recipe for dessert," according to Christa and Edwin, together four years and practically engaged in Boston, MA. "Espresso excites the blood. Dark chocolate puts the mind in the mood for love. And sweets made for dipping and sharing lend themselves to situations where the act of eating is only half the fun. The sweet meringues melt in your mouth almost like cotton candy. Once they're all eaten, the extra espresso cream can be enjoyed on its own – no spoons or bowls necessary, if you get my drift."

YIELDS 4 TO 6 SERVINGS

To make the meringue, preheat the oven to 200 degrees. Line a baking sheet with parchment paper. Sift the confectioners' sugar and granulated sugar together over a piece of waxed paper.

Combine the egg whites with a pinch of salt in a large mixing bowl. Beat with an electric mixer until frothy. Add 2 tablespoons of the sifted sugar, and keep beating until the whites are stiff and shiny. Be careful not to overbeat, or the whites will start separating and dry out. Fold in the rest of the sugar with a rubber spatula, folding delicately but thoroughly, being careful not to deflate the mixture.

For a nice presentation, snip the corner off of a large, resealable plastic bag. Fit the corner with a ¾-inch pastry tip (a #9, to be exact). Fill with the egg whites. Pipe 3-inch-long lengths onto the parchment paper at least 1 inch apart. They will look a bit like fat lady fingers. Or, pipe in a circular coil to create larger "plates" of meringue. Alternatively, if you don't have a pastry tip, fill a large, resealable plastic bag with the egg whites and snip off one corner for piping. The presentation won't be as clean, but it will still work. For an even easier (if less refined) method, spoon dollops of meringue directly onto the parchment.

Bake the meringue for 2 hours. Turn off the oven and let the meringue dry out in the warm oven overnight, especially if you live in a humid climate. The meringues can be made weeks in advance and stored in an airtight container in a cool, dry place. (continued)

When the meringues are completely dry, melt the chocolate. Place the chocolate in a microwave-safe bowl and microwave — uncovered — at 50 percent power for 1 minute at a time, stirring in between each heating, until the chocolate is almost completely melted. (Be careful, as chocolate can scorch easily.) Remove the chocolate from the microwave when almost melted, and continue stirring to melt any remaining bits.

Brush the melted chocolate onto the flat bottom of the lady-finger-style meringues, or on top of the plate-style meringues. Place in the refrigerator to harden.

While the chocolate's setting, make the espresso cream. Place all the ingredients in a large mixing bowl and whip with an electric mixer until the espresso dissolves and the mixture forms soft peaks. Be sure to start with well-chilled cream, well-chilled beaters, and a well-chilled bowl, if possible. And don't overbeat, or you may end up with espresso butter instead.

There are a variety of ways to serve this dish. For little rounds of meringues, simply top with the cream. For the larger plates of meringue, slather with the cream and cut into wedges. For the lady fingers, pour the espresso cream into a beautiful serving bowl large enough to hold 2 servings. Stick 4 meringue fingers upright into the cream, and share with your partner, double-dipping until all the cream is gone.

b a s i l

Considered the royal herb of the Greeks and a sacred herb in India, the alluring power of basil has been used for centuries to keep wandering eyes focused homeward. Early on, says Vera Lee in *Secrets of Venus*, wives with straying husbands "powdered their breasts with pulverized basil." Haitian lore claims basil comes from Erzulie, their goddess of love. And today, some therapists use the essential oil of basil to treat the madonna/whore complex. • But it's more than its historical use that makes basil an aphrodisiac. It's the beauty of a healthy basil plant, with its buttery leaves painting a background of green for its white flowers. • Once picked, its fragrance seasons a plain strand of pasta, adds an unexpected dimension to a simple garden salad, and makes a frozen pizza almost edible. • Celebrate basil. Make a laurel of purple and green leaves dotted in basil flowers. Whirl up an obscene amount of pesto, filling numerous Mason jars to the brim — enough to bring several bursts of summer during the doldrums of winter. Serve an anticipatory dinner to test the efficacy of the pesto and/or the laurel.

grilled scallops with basil and lavender essence

simple ingredients, complex flavor

15 to 20 fresh basil leaves

1   clove garlic

1   teaspoon salt, plus more
    to taste

¼   teaspoon freshly ground
    black pepper

2   drops essential oil of lavender

2   tablespoons olive oil,
    divided

¾   pound sea scallops,
    preferably U/10 or
    10/20 count

To introduce your taste buds to a whole new realm of senses, consider incorporating essential oils into your cooking. Essential oil is just that – the very essence of a particular flower, plant, or other botanical. In this case, Spencer Krenke with Aromatherapy of Rome recommends adding lavender essence to the simple classic of sautéed scallops or shrimp for a complex mixture of flavors with each bite. To make sure they're pure flavors and not synthetic ones, be sure to buy only food-grade oils for cooking. See page 198 for a reputable resource.

Steer clear of scallops that look too perfectly white, as that most often indicates heavy soaking in phosphates. Milky liquid is another bad sign. Instead, look for natural-colored scallops, drier rather than wetter, with a briny smell of the sea.

YIELDS 2 TO 3 SERVINGS

Combine the basil, garlic, salt, and pepper in a food processor or blender; process until smooth. Add the 2 drops of lavender essential oil to 1 tablespoon of the olive oil, and then add to the processed mixture. Cover and chill for 30 minutes for the flavors to meld.

Prepare a hot grill or preheat the broiler. Holding the scallop flat against a cutting board, cut a deep slit into the edge of the scallop, being careful not to cut through to the other side. Gently pack a bit of the basil purée into the slit using your finger or a small spoon. Secure the scallop closed with a toothpick if the purée is seeping out. Once all the scallops are filled, drizzle them with the remaining tablespoon of olive oil and sprinkle with salt and pepper to taste.

Grill the scallops for 2 to 3 minutes on each side, or until golden brown on the outside and barely cooked in the center. (Alternatively, you can broil or sauté the scallops.) If using smaller scallops, consider using a grill basket to keep from losing any through the grate.

basil-eggplant soup

filling and hearty

After three years in the Peace Corps, Sam and Bev live quite the minimalist lifestyle. They operate in a fully-equipped kitchen, complete with one wooden spoon, one small paring knife, one stock pot, and a cast-iron griddle. Regardless, they found this recipe's taste well worth the cooking detours required by a life sans grill or blender. They enjoyed their soup from their tiny balcony, which, with the help of the nighttime stars, made for a quaint dining experience.

YIELDS 2 TO 3 SERVINGS

Preheat the oven to 400 degrees. Peel the eggplant and cut into large cubes. Place on a rimmed cookie sheet and drizzle with 1 tablespoon of the olive oil, sprinkle with salt and pepper to taste, and toss to distribute the oil. Roast for 40 to 50 minutes, or until cooked through, turning several times for even cooking. (Alternatively, prepare the eggplant in the microwave. Prick the unpeeled eggplant several times with the tines of a fork. Place the eggplant on a plate and microwave at full power for 8 to 10 minutes, or until tender throughout. Let cool until safe to handle, and then slice in half and scoop out the pulp.)

In a large saucepan set over medium-high heat, add 3 tablespoons of olive oil. Add the onion and sauté until translucent and tender. Add the garlic and sauté 1 to 2 minutes. Add the eggplant, tomatoes, chicken stock, oregano, and cayenne. Season with salt and pepper to taste. Simmer, partly covered, for 35 minutes. Taste and adjust seasonings if needed.

While the soup is cooking, purée the basil in a blender with the remaining 2 tablespoons oil. Place in a small bowl, and stir in the goat cheese.

In the same blender, pour in the eggplant mixture. Place a towel over the lid for safety and pulse the mixture until puréed. Add more hot stock if the soup seems too thick. Pour the soup into bowls and serve with a dollop of basil-chèvre purée.

1 medium eggplant (about 1 pound)

6 tablespoons olive oil, divided

   Salt and freshly ground black pepper to taste

1 small onion, finely minced

1 large clove garlic, crushed

1 can whole plum tomatoes, seeded and chopped

1½ cups chicken or vegetable stock, or more for a thinner soup

½ tablespoon dried oregano

   Pinch of cayenne pepper

1 cup packed fresh basil leaves

2 ounces goat cheese

basil and tomato confit

the aroma of summertime

3 cups loosely packed fresh
basil leaves

9 medium homegrown or
Roma tomatoes

3 cloves garlic, thinly sliced

¼ cup extra-virgin olive oil

Salt and freshly ground
black pepper to taste

½ cup freshly grated
Parmesan cheese

This dish is meant for the height of summer, when you're trying to figure out what to do with your bumper crop of tomatoes and basil. And what a solution it is: "Rick loved this – he put it on the risotto, he slathered it on the bread, he ate it plain. When I told him how much work it was to peel the tomatoes, he said, 'Who cares – it is so worth it.' And then he thanked me profusely. Since my daughter and her husband also tested recipes and will be reading our results as well, I best leave it at that."
Janey and Rick, married 36 years, El Dorado, AR

YIELDS 4 TO 6 SERVINGS

Preheat the oven to 350 degrees. Bring a large pot of water to a boil over high heat. Prepare a large ice bath. Blanch both the basil and tomato: Lower the basil in the boiling water with a skimmer for 5 seconds, and then immediately remove the leaves and plunge into the ice bath. (This will keep the basil from turning brown when baked.) Remove and blot dry. Peel the tomatoes by making an X at the base with a sharp knife. Drop the tomatoes into the same rapidly boiling water. As soon as the skin around the X starts curling up, 20 to 30 seconds, remove the tomatoes from the boiling water and plunge into the same ice bath. Peel and discard the skin.

Cut the tomatoes in half crosswise, remove the core on top, and squeeze out the seeds. In a baking dish large enough to hold the tomatoes in one layer (a standard 11 x 7 x 2-inch casserole will most likely work), arrange the basil leaves to cover the bottom of the dish. (If you didn't blanch the basil, it will look like a copious amount, but the leaves will cook down to a beautiful consistency.) Place the tomatoes, cut-side up, on the bed of basil. Place several slivers of garlic in each tomato. Drizzle the olive oil over the tomatoes and basil, and season with plenty of salt and pepper to taste.

Bake the tomatoes for 45 minutes, or until the tomatoes have completely fallen apart. Press the cooked tomatoes into the basil and olive oil with the back of a fork, and then return to the oven for another 15 minutes. The tomatoes may start to brown lightly at the end of cooking. Serve over your favorite pasta or bruschetta with freshly shaved Parmesan.

basil frittata hero

egg sandwich extraordinaire

"If thou dost love fair Hero, cherish it, . . .
And thou shalt have her." Don Pedro, *Much Ado About Nothing*

YIELDS 2 SERVINGS

Preheat the broiler. Combine the eggs, milk, salt, and pepper in a large mixing bowl, and whisk until well combined. Set a medium-size, oven-safe sauté pan over medium heat and add the oil. Sauté the garlic and onions for 2 to 3 minutes, or until the shallot has softened. Pour in the egg mixture and sprinkle with the basil. Stir one or two times to release the cooked egg from the pan and allow the uncooked egg to flow to the bottom. When the eggs are almost cooked, but still have a thin layer of liquid on top, sprinkle with the Parmesan and place under the broiler. (If using the soft Swiss cheese wedges, reserve for the bread.) Broil for 3 to 4 minutes, or until the frittata is puffed and the cheese has browned. Remove from the oven and turn out on a plate. Cut into wedges or slices that fit the bread.

While the frittata is cooking, grill the bread. Set a large skillet over medium-high heat. Slice the rolls half lengthwise and spread with unsalted butter. Place, butter-side down, on the hot skillet and cook until warmed through and golden brown.

To assemble the sandwiches, spread with mayonnaise (or the soft Swiss cheese wedges), place the frittata on the bread, layer with a few leaves of spinach, and top with the other half of the grilled bread. Slice in half and serve immediately.

5 large eggs

3 tablespoons milk

Salt and freshly ground black pepper to taste

1 tablespoon olive oil

1 clove garlic, minced

1 teaspoon minced shallot or onion

¼ cup julienned fresh basil leaves

¼ cup freshly grated Parmesan cheese or 2 wedges Laughing Cow Swiss cheese

2 French bread rolls

2 tablespoons unsalted butter, softened

2 tablespoons mayonnaise, if desired

Handful of fresh spinach leaves

tomato-basil soup

a heart-warmer

1 tablespoon olive oil

1 small onion, chopped

2 or 3 cloves garlic, thinly sliced

1 (14½-ounce) can chopped tomatoes

½ cup tomato sauce

¾ cup chicken or vegetable broth, or more to taste

2 tablespoons chiffonade of fresh basil

¼ cup heavy cream, if desired, or more to taste

Salt and freshly ground black pepper to taste

Store-bought pesto for garnish, if desired

Freshly grated Parmesan cheese for garnish

2 sliced rounds country bread, well toasted for croutons

John enjoyed his tomato-basil soup: "This luscious soup offered us everything we could ever want in a tasteful prelude to an amorous evening encounter: the wonderful smell of onions, garlic, and basil wafting through our home as they simmered; the smooth, rich texture and warm layers of flavor cascading from lips to tongues to throats, then bellies. Finally, the surprisingly sensuous effect of good French bread (try sourdough!), soaked through with velvety, herb-laden liquid, giving nourishing sustenance to a light, energizing meal. Afterward: untold delights."

YIELD 2 TO 3 SERVINGS

Set a large saucepan over medium-high heat and add the oil. Sauté the onion until translucent. Reduce the heat and add the garlic. Sauté until the onion begins to soften, and then add the tomatoes, tomato sauce, and broth. Let simmer for 15 minutes.

For a chunky soup, process with an immersion blender for a few seconds just to break up the tomato pieces. For a completely smooth soup, process in a blender and strain through a fine sieve. Stir in half the basil and the cream. Add more cream for a more decadent soup, less for a lighter version. Place over low heat just to warm through. Season with salt and pepper to taste.

Ladle into soup bowls, garnish with the remaining basil or a dollop of pesto, fresh shavings of Parmesan cheese, and a crusty crouton on the side.

summertime cucumber sandwiches

light and cool for sultry days

These sandwiches go with lemonade and front porches. First kisses and hot days. Ceiling fans and tree swings. Picnics and wildflowers. They can take you back to the days of innocence and discovery, when Mom made cucumber sandwiches for you and the boy down the street, and he touched your hand while she trimmed the final crust from the bread. *[Update: Okay, the boy down the street would never dare to touch your hand with your mother standing there. Smile, maybe. Touch, never. But damn, these sandwiches are good, even if this headnote is a little wistful and sappy.]*

YIELDS 6 SMALL SANDWICHES

Place the sliced cucumbers on a paper towel and top with another paper towel to absorb some of their liquid. Combine the mayonnaise, sour cream, vinegar, salt, pepper, chopped basil, parsley, dill, chives, onions, Tabasco, and Worcestershire sauce in a small bowl. Mix well. (The spread can be made up to 2 days ahead, covered, and chilled.)

   To assemble the sandwiches, spread a thin layer of the mayonnaise-herb mixture on each slice of bread. Place several layers of thinly sliced cucumbers on half of each sandwich. Place 2 basil leaves on top of the cucumbers, and then top with another slice of bread. Cut into triangles and serve immediately.

1   cucumber, peeled and very thinly sliced

¼   cup mayonnaise

¼   cup sour cream

1   teaspoon cider vinegar
    Salt and freshly ground black pepper to taste

1   teaspoon each chopped fresh basil, parsley, dill, and chives

1   teaspoon minced onion

¼   teaspoon Tabasco
    Dash of Worcestershire sauce

12   slices white bread, crusts removed

12   fresh basil leaves

paws up
icy basil lemonade

pucker up, sweetie

Nothing is more thirst-quenching than homemade lemonade — except lemonade enhanced by a few gently crushed basil leaves. I first tasted this on 37,000 acres of God's country in Montana at The Resort at Paws Up. They have several incarnations of the drink, one involving lemongrass that will make you never, ever want to leave their resort. (Never mind the green rolling hills, bald eagles flying overhead, horses enjoying the grass, and expansive blue sky stretching beyond the snow-capped mountains in the distance.) After you've gotten all heated up from these thoughts of Montana, cool yourself down with an icy pitcher of this lemonade. Use superfine sugar, which dissolves much more easily than regular granulated sugar, and make sure the basil is very fresh — not wilted or blackened.

"It is one of those sticky July nights at the tail end of a heat wave. The kind of night where the thickness of the air makes me dreamy for childhood summers . . . for that old, jittery excitement of being out after dark . . . the feel of my bare feet sinking into damp grass.

"We are standing in my tiny New York kitchen, David and I, and the last of the day's heat is lolling through the apartment like some enormous, lazy cat. David has already peeled his T-shirt over his head, and he is hovering over my little ledge of counter, wiping at his furrowed brow. He is concentrating on smashing the basil. His long, freckled fingers dip into the sugary mess in the bowl, gently crushing at the leaves, and the lush smell that rises up seems to fill the room with the promise of some faraway paradise . . . someplace with towering trees and spongy riverbanks — or at the very least, more counter space and central air.

"I clink ice into two tall glasses. David pours the whole concoction into a pitcher and tips the spout for each of us. The tart shock of the drink twists my lips into a little O. Outside, a car blasts its horn, and the muddled music from a neighbor's television sings its way through the window. David brings his wet mouth down to mine, and the sweetness in his kiss makes my bare feet curl against the tiles. This is summer in the city, and it is delicious." *Johanna and David, dating 10 months, Brooklyn, NY*

"Refreshing, tasty, different, just wonderful. Floating thin slices of lemon in the pitcher make for a summery presentation, and rubbing some basil around the rim of the glasses gives you that basil taste a split second before your tongue tastes the lemon." *Roger and Christy, Jersey City, NJ* (continued)

In a medium-size, nonreactive bowl, combine the lemon juice and sugar and stir until the sugar has dissolved. Wash the basil leaves very carefully, then add them to the lemon-sugar mixture and gently crush the leaves against the sides and bottom of the bowl, using the back of a spoon or, better, a cocktail muddler. Taste the mixture; if you desire a stronger basil flavor, add more leaves and crush.

Pour the mixture into a large glass pitcher, add the water, and stir. Serve in tall glasses filled with ice cubes, and save some for later, post-bedroom workout. For a bit of bubbly, top each glass with a splash of effervescent seltzer water. Or, for an over-21-only drink, add ¾ ounce (about 1½ tablespoons) citron vodka or Limoncello to each glass, pour in the lemonade, and stir.

1   cup freshly squeezed
    lemon juice

1   cup superfine sugar

8   large or 12 medium-size
    fresh basil leaves, or more
    if desired

1   quart water

sugared basil tuile cups with lemon sorbet

you can even eat the dishes

6 tablespoons unsalted
   butter, cubed

¾ cup sugar

⅓ cup plus 2 tablespoons
   all-purpose flour

¼ teaspoon vanilla extract

¼ teaspoon lemon extract

2 large egg whites

1 tablespoon finely grated
   lemon zest

¾ teaspoon dried basil

1 tablespoon freshly squeezed
   lemon juice

   Lemon sorbet

8 leaves fresh basil for garnish

These sugary/savory tuile cups, formed from still-warm cookies, make lovely, edible vessels in which to serve store-bought lemon sorbet. The tuiles can be made ahead – ideal for an aphrodisiac meal – and its sophisticated look and flavor will wow your paramour.

YIELDS 6 TO 8 SERVINGS

Cream the butter and sugar together in a food processor for about 10 seconds, or until crumbly and the size of small peas. Add the flour, vanilla extract, lemon extract, and egg whites. Pulse another 10 seconds to a thickened liquid. Pour into a mixing bowl and stir in the lemon zest, lemon juice, and basil. Cover and refrigerate at least 1 hour or preferably overnight to let the batter rest.

Preheat the oven to 400 degrees. Set aside 4 drinking glasses for shaping the cookie "bowls." Line 2 baking sheets with parchment paper. Cut the paper in half for easy removal of each tuile after baking. Scoop 1 tablespoon of the batter and pour onto one of the halves of parchment. Using the back of the measuring spoon, spread the batter into a 5-inch circle. (Start from the middle, and use circular motions to spread the batter outward.) Repeat for 3 remaining cookies, placing 1 on each half of parchment.

Bake for 5 to 7 minutes, or until golden brown. Watch carefully, as these thin cookies can move from under-cooked to burned in just a moment's time. Remove from the oven. While the cookies are still very warm — and being careful not to burn your fingers — set the bottom of one of the glasses in the center of a cookie. Pick up the parchment and carefully invert the cookie over the bottom of the glass so that it drapes down. Remove the parchment, and shape the cookie gently with your hands to form an upside-down bowl; let cool. Repeat the process for a second batch of 4 cookies. When cool, fill each tuile with 1 scoop of lemon sorbet, and garnish with a basil leaf.

white bean dip
with basil-infused oil

creamy white in a clear pool of vibrant green

Creating the infused-oil dressing for this otherwise simple bean dip involves a bit of work — including straining the oil twice — but it's worth the effort to create a clear, green-tinted oil. The finished dip's flavor has a summery, herbal freshness reminiscent of homemade pesto, and it's even better on day two. See page 199 for some truly edible massage oils, though I suspect the basil oil might be nice dotted on your pulse points, with a fresh sprig of basil tucked behind your ear for extra flair.

YIELDS 6 APPETIZER SERVINGS

½ cup fresh basil leaves, tightly packed

¼ cup plus 3 tablespoons extra-virgin olive oil, divided

1 (15½-ounce) can cannellini or other white beans

1 small clove garlic, crushed and coarsely chopped

1 teaspoon freshly squeezed lemon juice

½ teaspoon freshly ground black pepper

Salt to taste

To keep the basil bright green, blanch and shock it: Fill a large saucepan with water and bring to a boil. Meanwhile, fill a large bowl with water and 2 or 3 trays' worth of ice cubes. Place the basil in a strainer and lower it into the boiling water for 5 seconds, making sure all the leaves are covered. Immediately transfer the basil to the ice-water bath. Drain the basil and transfer it to a bed of paper towels, wrapping the towels around the leaves and squeezing them to remove as much water as possible. Combine the basil and ¼ cup of the oil in a blender and pulse until the leaves are very finely chopped. Pour the mixture through a fine-mesh sieve into a measuring cup or other spouted vessel. Then, for an even clearer oil, pour it through 6 to 8 layers of cheesecloth into a small pitcher. Refrigerate until ready to use.

Drain the beans, reserving the liquid. Place the beans, 3 tablespoons of the oil, the garlic, lemon juice, pepper, and salt in a blender. Add 2 tablespoons of the reserved liquid from the beans and pulse until the mixture is smooth. If it is too dry, add more of the reserved liquid, 1 tablespoon at a time, until it has the consistency of mayonnaise. Transfer the dip to a shallow bowl, cover, and let stand for 1 hour. (You may refrigerate it if you wish.)

When ready to serve, use a spoon to make a small well in the center of the dip. Pour the infused oil into this well and, using a chopstick or the handle of the spoon, draw the oil in a spiral pattern over the surface of the dip. Serve with potato or vegetable chips.

g r a p e s

Try to imagine a world without grapes. Certainly, some substitutions will work. No more home-canned muscadine jelly for your buttermilk biscuits? Try strawberry jam. No more rich juice to sip? Apple will suffice. • No more pale-green, ruby-red, or midnight-purple clusters for the artist's still life? Pears are pretty. No more grape vine to swirl about your fresh-cut flowers? How about some wheat stalks or ferns?

• No more Chardonnay or Beaujolais or Pinot Noir or port or Champagne or sherry or vermouth? That's okay, you can distill some elderberries in your back yard. • No more plump bites of juice and sweet that squirt a fountain of aphrodisiacal power and grape flavor into your mouth? That's right. No more. • Oh, to shudder at the thought of such a sad existence. Savor your grapes. Appreciate them well.

quail braised with grapes

rich with pancetta, cognac, and thyme

4 dressed quail

Salt and freshly ground black pepper

3 tablespoons olive oil

1 shallot, minced

5 thin slices pancetta, finely chopped

1 tablespoon chopped fresh thyme, plus several sprigs for garnish

2 tablespoons cognac or brandy

3/4 cup Pinot Grigio or other white wine

2½ cups seedless red or purple grapes

Red wine vinegar or freshly squeezed lemon juice, if needed

Honey, if needed

1 tablespoon unsalted butter, chilled

This recipe was tested by two couples, one together only 10 months – and still in that sensual frenzy that can rarely be replicated later in the relationship. Danielle and Asher, on the other hand, tested the recipe after three years together. Their results feel completely different, but just as good.

After eight years with my own partner, Jeff, the intensity has lessened, but so has the angst. Beneath the passion, we have a warm, comforting glow, not the orange-hot fire of the earlier days. What will we feel after 12 years? After 25 years?

I just returned from a cruise where our dining partners were celebrating 34 years of marriage. Their last child was about to leave the house, and they were each entering "retirement lite." They have a whole other life awaiting them, with the allure of more golf time for Vince, theater time for Carla, and travel time together. They took swing dance classes with us, laughed at each other's jokes, and shared an obvious and deep affection for one another. What will they feel at the 50-year mark? I'm excited for them to find out.

"The tender meat was best eaten with fingers. Nibbling and tearing our way through a decadent repast, we eyed each other hungrily. After the last bird was finished, the last grape gone, and the last finger licked clean, we had dessert on the table, on the chair, and on the floor." *Nate and Keyana, together 10 months, London, England*

"Though I have eaten quail once or twice in my life, I have never actually touched the little guys, and I have to admit, it was quite a different tactile experience. My boyfriend and I both added the spices to the quail with our hands, and cooked together, which we rarely do. (Usually I drink a glass of wine and just watch him.) That was a very romantic thing to do together, but not as romantic as eating the quail, which had a lovely sauce, particularly good for the dipping of bread. We ate by candlelight, with medieval music playing, and I truly felt I was living in some French castle of centuries ago." *Danielle and Asher, together 3 years, Brooklyn, NY*

YIELDS 2 SERVINGS

Rinse the quail and pat thoroughly dry. Season well with salt and pepper. Set a large, heavy, ovenproof skillet over medium heat. Add the oil. Add the quail, 2 at a time, and brown on all sides. Don't rush the browning process, as this is what creates the tasty fond, or drippings, that add such flavor to the sauce. Remove the birds to a plate; they will not be cooked through. (continued)

Preheat the oven to 350 degrees.

Adjust the burner to medium, and add the shallot and pancetta, cooking until the shallot is translucent and the pancetta is beginning to crisp. Add the thyme, stirring to coat with the fat and release its flavor. Increase the heat to high and add the cognac, scraping the bottom of the pan with a wooden spoon to release any flavorful bits. Stir in the wine and simmer 1 to 2 minutes. Stir in the grapes. Place the quail, breast-side up, and any of its juices into the pan.

Cover and place in the oven. Braise for 15 to 20 minutes, or until the quail is cooked through and its juices run clear. Remove the pan from the oven and return to the stove top. Place the quail on a serving platter. Bring the sauce to a boil and let it reduce slightly. While its reducing, taste the sauce, and adjust the seasonings if necessary. If it seems too sweet, add a few drops of red wine vinegar or a squirt of lemon for a bit of acidity. If it seems too sour, add a bit of honey until the desired sweetness is reached. When reduced to the desired consistency, turn off the heat and swirl in the butter for a silky finish to the sauce. Pour over the quail and garnish with sprigs of fresh thyme. Feel free to eat them with your fingers if you like. Messy is not always bad. Serve with mashed potatoes or crusty bread to soak up any extra juices.

Henry and I couldn't believe it. As the recipe instructs, I prepared the pasta last, and served it immediately (with garlic breadsticks, Gamay Beaujolais, and sliced garden tomatoes). The meal was wonderful, very romantic. Lots of talking and long glances over the table full of luminous dishes. We had both eaten quite a bit more than we were known to, and had just leaned back in our chairs to relax, finish the wine, and exchange a languid smile, when a particularly slender piece of pasta stood up, bowed to a sprig of watercress (who, we think, responded with a curtsy) and began to dance the tango. It was rough going until they worked their way down the plate (away from the grapes, who were, at this point, very worked up and, with all their shimmying, had made the dance floor quite perilous) and onto the tablecloth. It was on the table that they really let loose, dipping, twirling, and seducing each other until they fell, exhausted, onto the butter plate in a fit of giggles and kisses.

Jen and Henry, on their amazing experience of *pasta with grapes*

sausages with grape sauce

plump links complemented by sweet grapes

As Susan tells it, "Once David quit making jokes about the sausage links and started tasting them instead, the evening turned round in my favor. I was at the stove and had just finished adding the grapes to the sauce. I dipped my finger in it for a taste test to adjust the seasonings, but he stopped my hand mid-route to my mouth. When he took it on a detour to his mouth, I knew it was going to be a good evening." *Susan and David, together 3 years, Anaheim, CA*

YIELDS 3 TO 4 SERVINGS

Preheat the oven to 200 degrees to keep the finished sausages warm. Set a large skillet over medium-high heat. Add the sausage links, browning on all sides. Pour a cup of water into the skillet, scraping the bottom to release any browned bits. Cover and cook until the water has evaporated and the sausages are cooked through.

Place the sausages in the oven to keep warm, reserving up to 1 tablespoon oil from the sausages in the skillet. If no oil remains, add the olive oil and sauté the shallot over medium heat until translucent and soft. Stir in the white wine, bring to a boil, and season with salt and pepper to taste. Reduce the heat to medium-low, whisk in the mustard, and stir in the grapes. To serve, spoon the sauce over the links and garnish with parsley.

4 links Italian sausage, or other good-quality, freshly made sausage (about 3/4 pound)

1 tablespoon olive oil, if needed

1 shallot, minced

1 cup dry white wine

Salt and freshly ground black pepper to taste

1 tablespoon Dijon mustard

1/2 cup seedless grapes, halved

1 1/2 tablespoons minced fresh parsley

cabernet sauvignon ice

luscious, ruby-red dessert

½ cup water

½ cup sugar

¾ cup Cabernet Sauvignon

¾ cup white grape juice

⅓ cup freshly squeezed
lemon juice

Champagne grapes
for garnish

Fresh mint sprigs
for garnish

"We had just taken Mollie, our two-year-old black lab, for a walk on the banks of the Mississippi near our house. She exudes life and expects everyone to come along with her – even when it's 90 degrees with 90 percent humidity. When she finally wore out (long after we had worn out), she allowed us to return home to our ceiling fan, slingback chairs, and Cabernet Sauvignon ice from the night before. The refreshingly non-sweet slush just about sent us over the edge. We ended up sitting in our slingbacks, talking and sipping the snowflakes of ice until the sun went down over the river."
Marilyn and Tom, married 26 years, Memphis, TN

YIELDS 2 TO 3 SERVINGS

Combine the water, sugar, and wine in a saucepan set over high heat. Bring to a boil. Reduce the heat and simmer for 5 minutes. Remove from the heat and stir in the grape juice and lemon juice. Let cool, and then pour into a divided ice cube tray. Cover with plastic wrap so that the syrup doesn't pick up other flavors from the freezer. Freeze until solid, about 4 hours. (If the temperature is just so, the ice cubes will have beautiful crystals splintering off through them.)

Place the cubes, in small batches, in a food processor. Process until just slushy. Serve in sherbet dishes garnished with champagne grapes and a sprig of mint.

grapes rolled in almonds and ginger

addictive, pop-in-your-mouth spheres

Concerning these voluptuous jewels, Jim wrote, "Laurel said this one was fun – need I say more? If we can get her smiling, the road to ecstasy is not far away." (Especially if you can find all the ingredients quickly, as may not be the case for those unfamiliar with crystallized ginger. Also known as candied ginger, it is ginger that has been saturated and coated with sugar. You can find it in most supermarket produce, spice, or bulk sections.)

YIELDS 2 SERVINGS

Chop the toasted almonds finely or grind in a food processor. Blend the cream cheese and ginger in a bowl with an electric mixer. Stir the grapes into the cream cheese mixture to coat. Roll the grapes in the ground almonds. Place on a waxed-paper-lined plate and chill until firm.

½ cup whole almonds, toasted

1 (3-ounce) package cream cheese, softened

1 tablespoon finely chopped crystallized ginger

15 to 20 seedless grapes, washed and thoroughly dried

pasta with grapes

fruit and cheese plate meets pasta

Give your partner a quick jolt of Mae West seduction and peel them grapes!

YIELDS 3 SERVINGS

Bring a large pot of salted water to a boil. Cook the pasta according to package directions until just al dente. Drain and toss with the remaining ingredients. Serve hot, room temperature, or chilled.

6 ounces pasta spirals

2 ounces goat cheese, cut into small wedges

4 ounces seedless white grapes

1 bunch watercress, trimmed and coarsely shredded

2 scallions, chopped

Juice and zest of ½ orange

Salt and freshly ground black pepper to taste

2 tablespoons olive oil

s t r a w b e r r i e s

"L'image que tu m'as envoyée a aiguisé mon goût pour . . . les fraises."
"The picture you sent me has heightened my taste for . . . (delicious pause) . . . strawberries."
A French friend, in response to his first glance of the strawberry image.

These fruits, rivaled only by the smooth cherry in innate sensuality, come as the harbinger of summertime. In the wild, the mix of tart and sweet red berries dots the landscape, swirling and twirling in a thicket of glory. In the store, they come packed by the carton, shoppers peering carefully through each clear box in hopes of finding the perfect, the red, the ultimate in strawberries. • Not a bad choice for an evening of seduction, the strawberry has a green button top that fits easily betwixt fingers. And more importantly, a berry that fits even more easily between parted lips. • Imagine for just one moment your partner as a strawberry, lightly dusted with confectioners' sugar or slowly dipped in warm, creamy chocolate. Or just enjoy your lover as we most often do the strawberry — plain and, at its essence, beautifully ripe.

easy strawberry empanadas

creamy, sweet, and flaky all rolled into one

1/4 cup cream cheese, room temperature

4 tablespoons light brown sugar, divided

2/3 cup coarsely chopped fresh strawberries

1 (8-count) package refrigerated crescent rolls

2 tablespoons unsalted butter, melted

"Make sure you crimp the edges together well because there's no way you want to lose any of that warm, creamy filling. We ate ours in the living room, feet up on the couch, with our favorite Nat King Cole songs playing in the background. Unforgettable." *Marilyn and Tom, married 26 years, Memphis, TN [Update: Marilyn and Tom are still together, but they've moved from the banks of the mighty Mississippi to the temperate climes of sunny LA. Ironically, their Memphis house and now their LA home sit atop the biggest fault lines in the country. Fortunately, the only thing that shakes is their bed. Did I just say that? Unforgettable indeed.]*

YIELDS 4 EMPANADAS

Preheat the oven to 375 degrees. Blend the cream cheese and 2 tablespoons of the brown sugar in a bowl. Fold in the strawberries.

Unfold the crescent roll dough into 4 rectangles, smoothing the dough together along the diagonal dotted line. Divide the strawberry mixture among the 4 pieces, spooning onto the bottom half of the rectangle. Fold the dough over and crimp the edges with your fingers or the tines of a fork.

Bake the rolls for 10 to 12 minutes, or until golden brown. Brush the cooked empanadas with melted butter, and dust with the remaining brown sugar before serving.

"My husband couldn't get enough of it! He liked the sauce too."

Diane, in response to her husband's reaction to strawberry butter sauce served over grilled fish. Diane and Dave, married 4 years, Cincinnati, OH

Serve *strawberry butter sauce* over broiled or grilled fish. Prepare by puréeing 1 (8-ounce) package frozen strawberries, 1 tablespoon ginger, and 1 ounce rum. Melt 2 tablespoons butter over medium heat. Stir in 1 tablespoon flour. Cook for 1 minute, stirring constantly. Add the strawberry purée. Cook for 5 minutes, stirring constantly.

strawberry-avocado salad

a perfect summer salad

¼ cup raspberry vinegar

1½ tablespoons sugar

¼ teaspoon hot sauce

¼ teaspoon salt

⅛ teaspoon freshly ground
black pepper

¼ teaspoon cinnamon

¼ cup olive oil

½ head romaine, torn into
bite-size pieces (3 to 4 cups)

½ (11-ounce) can Mandarin
oranges, drained

1 cup strawberries, stemmed
and quartered

½ cup sliced red onion
(about ½ small onion)

¼ cup coarsely chopped
pecans, toasted

½ avocado, sliced

"Our first attempt at the strawberry-avocado salad ended in blissful failure. Wilted lettuce. Brown avocado. Burnt pecans. When we were asked by our over-eager friends the next day how everything went, we could only shrug – red stained fingers momentarily hiding our strawberry-swollen lips."
Sophie and Dustin, newlyweds, Atlanta, GA

YIELDS 2 TO 3 SERVINGS

Combine the vinegar, sugar, hot sauce, salt, pepper, and cinnamon in a jar with a tight-fitting lid. Shake well. Pour in the olive oil and shake vigorously to mix well. Refrigerate for at least 30 minutes (and up to 3 days) to let the flavors meld while you prepare the rest of the salad.

In a large serving bowl, toss the lettuce with one-fourth of the dressing, or more if needed to coat lightly. Combine the oranges, strawberries, onion, pecans, and avocado in a separate bowl. Gently toss with another fourth of the dressing and scatter on top of the lettuce. Serve any remaining dressing on the side.

white chocolate and strawberry trifle

decadent layers

"I invited him over for dinner. I really didn't know what to expect. I wasn't feeling real sexy before he got there. I'm not the best cook in the world, so I was a little frantic trying to get everything to come out right. But I guess the planets were aligned correctly because everything was perfect. The entrée didn't burn, he showed up on time — a first — with flowers and bottle of wine in hand, and the white chocolate and strawberry trifle convinced him that he didn't need to leave quite as soon as he had planned." *Sarah, commenting on dessert and her 3-month dating relationship with Daniel, Jackson, MS*

YIELDS 4 TO 6 SERVINGS

Mix the sugar and egg yolks in a blender for 1 minute. Add the vanilla and blend 1 minute. Add the cream cheese and blend until smooth.

Beat the whipping cream to soft peaks in a large mixing bowl with an electric mixer. Add the cream cheese mixture to the whipped cream and fold together to combine gently. Cover and refrigerate while preparing the remaining ingredients.

Cut the cake into ½-inch slices and cut in half vertically. Dip the strips in the hot espresso, making sure each slice is thoroughly soaked. In a trifle bowl or decorative clear bowl, layer half the cake strips, white chocolate, cream cheese mixture, and strawberries. Repeat the layers with the remaining ingredients. Cover and chill until ready to serve.

⅓ cup sugar

2 large egg yolks

¾ teaspoon vanilla extract

1 (3-ounce) package cream cheese, softened

½ cup heavy whipping cream, chilled

4 ounces pound cake

1 teaspoon instant espresso, dissolved in ½ cup hot water

3 ounces high-quality white chocolate, shaved

¾ cup sliced strawberries (about ½ pint)

cornish hens with strawberry-balsamic sauce

perfect little birds

for the hens:

2 Cornish game hens, rinsed well and patted dry

2 tablespoons olive oil

Salt and freshly ground black pepper to taste

for the sauce:

½ cup seedless strawberry jam

1½ teaspoons balsamic vinegar

1 tablespoon white wine

⅛ teaspoon freshly ground black pepper

Salt to taste

1 dried Thai chile

To add a hint of exotica to the evening, Jim and Laurel suggest renaming the dish "Pornish Game Hens." But they warn this recipe is not for the weak of heart – Jim prepared the dish following a long day at work for the both of them and, as he sadly laments, the timing just wasn't right for Pornish Game Hens.

"After Laurel fought to get her food off that little hen, she wasn't in the mood." Fortunately, he had some puréed strawberries left. Putting them to good use, he spoonfed them to Laurel until she regained her strength and, once again, felt the full effect of the strawberries on her libido. [*Update: When I called Jim and Laurel for an update, Jim's secretary said they were in Brazil (eating skewers of roasted beef, pork, and sausage). The time before that, they were on safari in Botswana (having Dutch-oven beef Wellington cooked in a hole in the ground). And the time before that, in central India (enjoying a vegetarian smorgasbord of dal, bhindi, palak, and gobi). I met Jim and Laurel on a bus tour of Austria when I was a teenager and they were in their mid-30s. To the fact that we took a group bus tour, I can only say, "Forgive us, we know not what we do." But that trip was their first foray overseas, and it gave them the bug. Since then, travel has become the most potent aphrodisiac in their 28-year marriage, where they taste new cultures, new foods, and new ways of looking at things, all the while reconnecting with one another. "We go to repair our bond, to reattach," says Jim. "We find out, once again, why we like each other."*]

YIELDS 2 OR 4 SERVINGS

Preheat the oven to 425 degrees. Rub the hens with olive oil and season generously, inside and out, with salt and pepper. Tie their legs together with kitchen twine. Place the hens, breast-side up, on a wire rack set over a baking sheet and roast until the juices run clear or a thermometer registers 165 degrees in the thigh, about 25 to 35 minutes.

While the hens are roasting, prepare the sauce. Combine the strawberry jam, vinegar, wine, pepper, and salt in a small saucepan set over medium heat. As the jam begins to melt, add the Thai chile and let steep for 5 minutes. Taste the sauce; if you prefer something spicier, cut the chile in half and stir the sauce to distribute the fire. Remove the pepper when the desired spiciness is reached. Serve as a sauce for the roasted hens.

I break out in hives. It's not a food allergy. It's the pure excitement of the luscious scarlet fruit tempting my tongue. And his luscious tongue tempting my scarlet fruit.

Leila comments on her berry fetish

strawberries drenched in honeyed cream

basil infuses the cream with a hint of clove

½ cup packed fresh
basil leaves

1 cup (½ pint) heavy
whipping cream

¼ cup water

1 tablespoon honey

½ teaspoon vanilla extract

1 pint ripe strawberries,
or combination of
fresh berries

This luscious recipe comes courtesy of Janet Hazen. It's a variation on a dish in her delightful little book, *Basil*, simplified for strawberry lovers like us.

"I thought this would be the connection we needed. Three kids under five, the youngest only a few months old. Succulent strawberries packing a sweet cream punch. But like the spit-up still on my sleeve, I think I curdled the recipe. Life just needs to slow down. And when it does in the next couple of months, I'll pull this recipe out again, and this time we'll take it nice and slow, heating things up to the point of no return, till the cream runneth over." *Cale and Tom, together 8 years, married 6, Wenham, MA*

"We lay on our sides in my bed, the bowls of strawberries and cream balanced carefully between us on the sheets. I have purposely cued up embarrassingly cheesy make-out music on my stereo, and the scene we have set seems plucked straight from some sappy daytime soap. We eye each other warily in the dim light, waiting to see who is going to break first. David reaches into the bowl and pinches a fat berry between two fingers. He arches his eyebrows dramatically and moves the fruit slowly toward my lips. But the sight is too much . . . I can't take it anymore, and I am rolling toward the wall in laughter. I try to collect myself, and roll back to him – just in time to see him swallowing the remains of the berry. "You fed it to yourself?!?" I am incredulous. "Well you were taking too long to turn back around . . ." he tries to defend himself. David smiles and watches me laugh, calmly jamming another strawberry into his own mouth. Later, when the bowls are empty, I'm not sure if my belly is sore from laughter or from so much heavy cream. But when David pulls me to him, I smile into the stubble of his cheek, and the warmth that spreads through me is far sweeter than any dessert." *Johanna and David, dating 10 months, Brooklyn, NY*

YIELDS 2 SERVINGS

Coarsely tear all the basil, leaving a few pretty sprigs for garnish. Set a large, heavy saucepan over medium-high heat and pour in the cream, water, and honey. Bring to a boil, stirring frequently to keep the mixture from boiling over. Add the torn basil to the cream mixture, and reduce the heat to medium-low. Cook for 20 minutes, or until the cream is thick and pale brown. Add the vanilla and mix well. Strain through a fine sieve into a clean saucepan. Keep warm until ready to use.

Hull and stem the strawberries, and slice them into halves or quarters, depending on their sizes. To serve, place the berries in individual serving bowls and spoon with the warm, honeyed cream. Garnish with a fresh basil leaf and serve.

grand marnier strawberries over country biscuits

praise the lard and pass the biscuits

"As a born-and-bred Southern girl, I'm here to tell you that the perfect biscuit will warm any man's heart. Pair that with all the juiciness and ripeness a strawberry encompasses, and you've got a virtual feast that will bring you lovin' breakfast, lunch, and supper. Rest assured, this will feed you body and soul any time of day or night. It's the kind of treat that makes a couple who has been together literally half of their lives want to come back for more – not only at the table, but wherever we please! There's something magical about the sinfully sweet, liquor-infused berries with the melt-your-heart goodness of a biscuit. Topping this dish (and each other!) with cream will take it – and your partner – to a new level." *"B", who's been cooking her way into Jay's heart since their 9th-grade homecoming dance, married now 13 years, Memphis, TN*

YIELDS 10 TO 12 BISCUITS

Heat the preserves in a small saucepan on medium-low to liquefy. Remove from the heat and stir in the Grand Marnier. Add the strawberries, stirring gently to coat. (If used right away, the sauce will have a thicker consistency. If made ahead of time, the sauce will macerate the berries and have a more liquid consistency.) Whip the cream until soft peaks just begin to form. Add sugar, if desired, but the unsweetened cream tastes nice next to the syrupy berries.

For the biscuits, preheat the oven to 400 degrees. Line a baking sheet with parchment paper and grease the parchment with shortening. Combine the flour and baking powder with a fork in a large mixing bowl. Combine the buttermilk and the baking soda in a measuring cup, stirring well to combine. Cut the shortening into the flour mixture with a pastry cutter (or 2 table knives) until the butter is distributed throughout and is the size of coarse meal. Add the buttermilk to the shortening mixture and stir until just mixed.

Turn the dough out onto a floured surface, and knead 2 to 3 times just to bring the dough together. Flour your rolling pin well. Roll out the dough to a ¾-inch thickness. Cut out the biscuits with a 2½-inch circular cutter. Don't twist the cutter, as that crimps down the edges and may keep the biscuits from rising. Place the biscuits on the greased parchment and bake for 12 minutes, or until golden brown. Split open the hot-from-the-oven biscuits, spoon with the berries, and top with a spoon of the whipped cream.

for the strawberries:

- ½ cup strawberry preserves
- 2 tablespoons Grand Marnier
- 1 quart (or 2 pints) fresh strawberries, stemmed, hulled, and quartered
- ½ cup heavy whipping cream, chilled
- Sugar to taste (optional)

for the biscuits:

- ⅓ cup Crisco shortening, plus more for greasing
- 2 cups self-rising flour, preferably Dixie Lilly or Martha White
- 1½ teaspoons baking powder
- 1 cup low-fat (1%) buttermilk
- Scant ¼ teaspoon baking soda

h o n e y

From the *Kama Sutra* to the *Perfumed Garden* to the Bible, honey has been connected with love, sex, and sensuality extraordinaire since the beginning of time. • In the fifth century B.C., Hippocrates prescribed it for sexual vigor. Galen, the court physician to Marcus Aurelius, recommended he down a glass of thick honey mixed with almonds and pine nuts, difficult though it may be. Tradition in India calls for a bridegroom to receive honey on his wedding day. Newlyweds typically go on a honeymoon, a practice that stems from an ancient tradition of couples going into seclusion and drinking a honey concoction until the first new moon of their marriage. • Physiologically, honey provides the body with a very usable form of sugar that converts easily into energy. Psychologically, honey encompasses sensuality. The very word honey conjures up golden images of the dripping, sticky, viscous substance, of honeybees, of honeysuckle, of all things sweet. And why shouldn't it? It comes from the nectar of flowers, from orange blossoms and dandelions, from raspberries and clover, from springtime and buzzing bees.

honey-nut pie

richly flavored with citrus overtones

1 cup honey

1½ cups chopped walnuts

Zest from 1 large lemon
(about 1 tablespoon)

4 tablespoons dark rum

2 tablespoons dried
breadcrumbs

1 tablespoon sugar

2 (9-inch) circles refrigerated
pie dough, preferably
Pillsbury's Just Unroll!

1 large egg yolk

1 tablespoon milk

1 cup (½ pint) heavy
whipping cream, chilled

1 tablespoon superfine sugar

"You are my honey, honeysuckle, I am the bee." When Randall saw this quote from Albert Fitz's 1901 song, he immediately thought of his grandparents, Valley and Lawrence. The story goes something like this: Lawrence and his brother, native Iowans, needed work and wives. They trekked around the country, doing odd jobs to support their main quest for love, until they came to a small town in Arkansas where Lawrence met Valley. He must have wooed her well, because she moved with him back to Iowa, where they married and began their family. Lawrence made his living as a beekeeper, always supplying Valley with honey galore. Valley loved Lawrence, Lawrence loved Valley, the bees loved Lawrence (he never once received a sting), and they both loved honey. Valley and Lawrence lived a full marriage of 69 happy years, and Randall will always remember them for their honey-sweet love.

YIELDS 6 SERVINGS

Preheat the oven to 400 degrees. Heat the honey in a small saucepan. Add the walnuts and lemon peel. Simmer until the mixture is hot and the walnuts are well-coated with honey. Remove from the heat and stir in the rum.

Spread the breadcrumbs and sugar on the bottom of a pie crust. (If you prefer to make a homemade crust, see page 162 for directions.) Spoon in the honey mixture. Top with the other pie crust. Seal the edges. Prick the top of the dough to let steam escape. Mix the egg yolk and milk in a small bowl. Brush over the top of the pie.

Bake for 30 to 40 minutes, or until the pastry is golden brown, covering with a foil shield if it's browning too quickly.

While the pie is baking, whip the cream in a large mixing bowl with an electric mixer or whisk until it begins to thicken. Sprinkle in the sugar, and continue beating until soft, fluffy peaks form. Be careful not to overbeat, or the cream will begin to separate and turn to butter. Remove the cake from the oven, cool, and serve with the whipped cream.

honey-almond delight

flaky niblets reminiscent of baklava

Mara has a crush on Jeff. Jeff works for Mara. She's never played the secret admirer, but she thought now might be the perfect time to start. First tactic? Honey-almond delight in kraft paper packaging with no return address. He liked it — ate the whole package in two days — but doesn't seem to have a clue as to the identity of his admirer. Next tactic? Mara says she's thinking of inviting him over for *Star Wars* and pizza, but will accidentally rent *Sense and Sensibility*. *Mara and Jeff, not yet together, Arlington, VA*

YIELDS 40 PIECES

Line a 15 x 10-inch jelly roll pan with foil. Place the flour, sugar, and salt in the bowl of a food processor. Pulse to combine. Add the chilled butter pieces and pulse just until the mixture resembles coarse meal.

Whisk the egg and almond extract in a small bowl. Add to the food processor and pulse until the dough starts to come together. Pour the mixture into the lined pan and pat with your hands, pushing the dough up the sides of the pan. Cover and refrigerate for 1 hour, or until ready to use.

Preheat the oven to 375 degrees. Prick the dough with a fork. Bake for 10 minutes, or until a light golden brown.

For the topping, combine the sugars, honey, and butter in a small saucepan set over medium heat. Bring to a simmer, and stir until the sugar dissolves and the butter melts. Increase the heat and bring to a boil. Cook for 3 minutes without stirring. Remove from the heat and stir in the cream and almonds. The mixture will be very thick. Spread the topping over the crust with a spatula. Bake for 10 to 15 minutes more, or until bubbly. Let cool, and then cut into triangles. Store in an airtight container for up to 4 days until ready to serve.

for the dough:

2¾ cups flour

½ cup sugar

½ teaspoon salt

½ pound (2 sticks) unsalted butter, cut into small cubes and chilled

1 large egg

¾ teaspoon almond extract

for the topping:

1 cup brown sugar

¼ cup sugar

⅓ cup honey

½ pound (2 sticks) unsalted butter, cut into pieces

¼ cup heavy cream

1 pound sliced almonds (about 5 cups)

king solomon: Your lips drop sweetness as the honeycomb, my bride; milk and honey are under your tongue . . . You are a garden locked up . . . you are a spring enclosed, a sealed fountain . . . a well of flowing water streaming down from Lebanon.

lover: Awake, north wind, and come, south wind! Blow on my garden, that its fragrance may spread abroad. Let my lover come into his garden and taste its choice fruits.

king solomon: I have come into my garden . . . my bride; I have gathered my myrrh with my spice. I have eaten my honeycomb and my honey; I have drunk my wine and my milk.

god: Eat, O friends, and drink; drink your fill, O lovers.

french toast baked in honey-pecan sauce

puffed clouds of ecstasy

This recipe offers the ultimate experience in French toast. For delectable results, stray not from the recipe, preparing it a day ahead with thick slices of day-old baguette. The eggs and cream and sweeteners saturate the bread overnight, then puff up to a golden, sticky ecstasy in the morning's hot oven.

YIELDS 2 TO 3 SERVINGS

Combine the eggs, half-and-half, brown sugar, and vanilla extract in a small bowl. Pour half the mixture into a baking dish. Place the bread in the pan and top with other half of the egg mixture, making sure all parts of the bread are saturated with the liquid. Refrigerate, covered, overnight.

Preheat the oven to 350 degrees. To melt the butter, place in a 13 x 9 x 2-inch baking dish and set in the oven. When melted, stir in the brown sugar, honey, maple syrup, and pecans. Set the soaked bread slices on top of the pecan mixture. Bake for 30 to 35 minutes, or until puffed and golden brown. Remove with a spatula and invert each slice onto serving plates. Spoon any extra syrup and nuts on top.

Serve immediately with ice cold milk or piping hot coffee.

honey butter: For that extra something on your morning toast, make a batch of honey butter. It keeps up to 4 weeks and is simple to make. Just combine 1 stick softened butter, 2 cups honey, and 2 cups light brown sugar with an electric mixer or food processor. Store in a crock and chill until firm.

---

4 large eggs, beaten

3/4 cup half-and-half

1/2 tablespoon brown sugar

1 teaspoon vanilla extract

4 (2-inch-thick) slices day-old French bread or other crusty bread

1/4 cup (1/2 stick) unsalted butter, cut into pieces

1/4 cup brown sugar

1/4 cup honey

1/4 cup maple syrup

1/4 cup chopped pecans

lemon thyme madeleines

honeyed cakes that inspire the senses

13 tablespoons (1½ sticks plus 1 tablespoon) unsalted butter, plus more for greasing

All-purpose flour for dusting

1⅔ cup confectioners' sugar

½ cup plus 1 tablespoon all-purpose flour

½ cup finely ground almonds

6 large egg whites

1 tablespoon honey

¼ cup freshly squeezed lemon juice

Zest of 2 lemons

3 tablespoons finely chopped lemon thyme

The idea of including this recipe is not to conjure up some Proustian memory of the past, but instead to create what will become a memory worth reliving the next time you prepare them. You are setting the stage for things to come, so take care with the process and consumption – what you experience with this madeleine will be forever written into the landscape of your memory.

"But, when nothing subsists of an old past, after the death of people, after the destruction of things, alone, frailer but more enduring, more immaterial, more persistent, more faithful, smell and taste still remain for a long time, like souls, remembering, waiting, hoping, upon the ruins of all the rest, bearing without giving way, on their almost impalpable droplet, the immense edifice of memory." Proust

YIELDS 30 MADELEINES OR 48 MINI-MUFFINS

You'll need madeleine molds for this recipe, though you could always pour the batter into cornbread molds or cupcake tins. They won't have the same visual appeal as Proust's version, but they'll taste just as yummy. Whatever pans you use, butter and flour them well, getting into all the little creases where the madeleines are most likely to stick. Use a butter spray if you prefer.

Set a large saucepan over medium-high heat. Place the butter in the pan and let cook until it foams and just begins to turn golden brown, about 3 to 5 minutes. Remove immediately from the heat and pour into a small bowl to stop the cooking.

Sift the sugar and the flour together in a medium mixing bowl. Add the ground almonds, stirring to distribute. Place the egg whites in a large mixing bowl and beat with an electric mixture until frothy. Add the sugar mixture and fold into the whites. Pour in the browned butter, honey, and lemon juice. Add the lemon zest and lemon thyme, and beat to incorporate.

Pour the batter into the buttered and floured molds, filling them almost to the top. Cover and refrigerate at least 1 hour to let the batter set. Preheat the oven to 375 degrees. Bake the madeleines for 12 to 15 minutes, or until a light-golden color. Remove from the oven, lightly bang the pan to loosen the cakes, and invert to unmold. Cool slightly on a wire rack before serving, or cool completely before storing. The madeleines will keep for 2 to 3 days in an airtight container.

honeyed duck breast
with dried cherries

don't miss the prized, crispy skin

Sweet-and-sour sauces coupling vinegar and honey are increasingly popular, especially for fowl. The powerful, sultry flavor of balsamic vinegar is just right for duck breast, whose taste and texture are surprisingly reminiscent of roast beef. This recipe ups the sweetness ante by adding plumped dried cherries to the sauce. Debbie and Dave, longterm couple-turned-newlyweds in Grapevine, Texas, concur. "We loved the voluptuous pink breasts, thinly sliced and topped with the plumped cherries."

YIELDS 2 SERVINGS

In a small bowl, cover the cherries with ½ cup boiling water. Let them plump for 20 to 30 minutes. Examine the skin of the duck breast carefully, removing any pin feathers.

Heat the oil in a small nonstick frying pan (choose a pan with a lid) over medium-high heat. Place the duck breast in the pan, skin-side down, and sear until the fat begins to melt, 1½ to 2 minutes. Turn the breast to sear the other side. Add the shallots and cook until they become translucent, about 2 minutes. Turn the breast again. Add the remaining ingredients (including the cherries and their soaking liquid), bring to a simmer, then cover and reduce the heat to low. Cook until medium-rare, about 12 minutes.

Remove the duck breast to a cutting board, and let rest for 5 minutes. Meanwhile, raise the heat to high, bring the sauce to a boil, and cook until it is reduced by half and has the consistency of a thickened gravy.

Cut the duck breast crosswise into thin slices. Pour half the sauce onto each of two plates, divide the duck slices into two portions, and lay them on top of the sauce. Serve with baked, mashed sweet potato and a bitter green vegetable, such as the Baby Bok Choy with Black Bean Sauce, page 115.

¼ cup dried cherries

1 duck breast, skin on (12 to 14 ounces)

½ teaspoon olive oil

1 tablespoon shallots, minced

1 tablespoon balsamic vinegar

2 teaspoons honey

¼ teaspoon dried rosemary or 1 sprig fresh rosemary

Freshly ground black pepper to taste

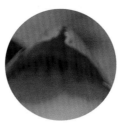

a r t i c h o k e s

Tough green leaves, each armed with its own thorn, stand on guard. They rally their strength to make one tightly woven bud, protecting the exquisite beauty found inside their walls. This aphrodisiac, like many lovers, plays hard to get (which, like many suitors, just makes one want it more). • Fortunately, some very hungry body figured out how to unleash the velvety softness found only in the stubborn artichoke. • Experience it for yourself: Together with your partner, insert your thumbs into the very center of a blanched artichoke, where the leaves meet. Slowly pull the petals apart and down. As the leaves fold down, they will reveal a veritable painting of green, white, and purple. Don't stop there, but delve deeper toward the center. Continue spreading the petals until you spy a hint of yellowy-white fur. Insert a finger into the opening. The fur, you will find, is protected by the prickly spears of the choke. But persevere, close your eyes, and stroke the velvety fur. • Or, if all this sounds too goofy, just steam the whole vegetable, dip in melted butter, and feed to your love.

artichoke muffaletta

easy twist on a new orleans classic

½ cup store-bought pesto

1 teaspoon Dijon mustard

½ loaf crusty French bread

1 cup artichoke hearts, thinly sliced

2 ounces provolone cheese, thinly sliced

1 small tomato, thinly sliced

1 cup (about 2 ounces) fresh spinach leaves

For a subliminally sexy sandwich, Jen and Henry recommend replacing the securing toothpicks with butcher's twine and tying up the muff. Get it really hot in a 350 degree oven. Remove the steaming, aromatic muff of melded spices drenched in melting cheese, then just dive in. Sure beats eating out, no?

Y I E L D S   2   S E R V I N G S

Combine the pesto and mustard in a small bowl; mix well. Cut the bread in half lengthwise. Hollow out the top half, leaving a 1-inch shell. (Dip the insides in the pesto, and eat on the spot.)

Spread the pesto mixture over each half. On one half, layer the artichokes, cheese, tomato, and spinach. Top with the other half. Cut crosswise into 3 or 4 pieces; secure with wooden picks. Wrap in butcher paper and go on a picnic.

baked artichoke and crab dip

an elegant alternative to chips and queso

½ tablespoon vegetable oil, plus more for greasing

1 small green bell pepper, chopped

1 (14-ounce) can artichoke hearts, drained and finely chopped

1 pickled jalapeño pepper, seeded and minced

1 cup mayonnaise

¼ cup thinly sliced scallions

¼ cup chopped pimiento

½ cup freshly grated Parmesan cheese

Juice of 1 small lemon

2 teaspoons Worcestershire sauce

½ teaspoon celery salt

½ pound crab meat, picked over for bits of shell

¼ cup sliced almonds, toasted

Serve this at a party where you're trying to play Cupid. The artichoke should send all arrows straight to the heart, making things a bit easier on you.

Y I E L D S   2   T O   3   S E R V I N G S

Preheat the oven to 375 degrees and grease a 6 x 9-inch baking dish. Set a small skillet over medium heat. Add the oil and sauté the bell pepper until tender.

Combine the artichokes, jalapeño, mayonnaise, scallions, pimiento, Parmesan cheese, lemon juice, Worcestershire sauce, celery salt, and sautéed bell pepper in a large bowl. Fold in the crab meat. Place the mixture in the baking dish and sprinkle with the almonds. Bake for 25 to 30 minutes, or until golden brown and bubbly. Serve with tri-colored tortilla chips.

broiled artichoke bottoms with chèvre and thyme

salty bits of prosciutto enhance each bite

You may be wondering if it's worth all your trouble to get to the bottom of a fresh artichoke. Indeed, it is. You start with this bulbous sticker bush. Then, with really not that much effort — anything involving a microwave can't be that much trouble — you've dealt with the stickers and hairy choke, and you're left with a smooth, delectable bottom. Once you've filled that bottom with creamy chèvre, aged prosciutto, and woodsy thyme, drizzled it with olive-green oil, and broiled it to a golden perfection, well, friend, if you can't make it happen with that, then I'm not sure you ever will.

Y I E L D S   4   S E R V I N G S

Trim off the stem so that the artichoke will sit flat on a plate. Snap off the really tough outer leaves around the base, if you like. Trim off the top third of the artichokes with a sharp knife. Wash the artichokes well, spreading the leaves slightly so the water can run through. Turn upside down and shake well.

Place the artichokes in a large, microwave-safe bowl and fill with about 1 inch of water. Cover and microwave about 6 to 8 minutes, and then let sit for another 10 minutes, still covered. Pull out a leaf. Taste it. If it pulls out easily and tastes soft, then it's done. If not, microwave the artichokes for a few more minutes.

To get to the artichoke bottoms from a whole, cooked artichoke, simply pull off the leaves, pull off the choke and discard, and slice off any remaining stem. (Don't discard the leaves. Rather, dip in vinaigrette and eat on the spot.) The artichokes can be steamed and plucked a day in advance. Wrap the artichoke bottoms in plastic and store in the refrigerator until ready to use.

Preheat the broiler. Combine the chèvre, prosciutto, and thyme in a small bowl with a fork until thoroughly mixed. Divide the cheese mixture evenly among the artichoke bottoms. Drizzle with the olive oil. Finish with a generous grind of fresh pepper. Place under the broiler for about 3 to 5 minutes, or until the artichokes are warmed through and the cheese has started to brown slightly and melt.

4 artichokes or 1 can artichoke bottoms

2 ounces chèvre (about 4 tablespoons), softened

2 thin slices prosciutto, minced

1 teaspoon fresh thyme leaves, chopped, or ½ teaspoon dry

2 tablespoons extra-virgin olive oil

Freshly ground black pepper to taste

artichoke potato salad

gourmet picnic fare

1 pound unpeeled small new potatoes, scrubbed and cubed

1 large egg

½ pound bacon

¼ cup mayonnaise

½ tablespoon red wine vinegar

Juice of ½ lemon

½ tablespoon Dijon mustard

1½ teaspoons minced fresh dill

1 teaspoon fresh lemon thyme leaves

Freshly ground black pepper to taste

3 tablespoons thinly sliced green onion, green and white parts

½ (9-ounce) jar marinated artichoke hearts, drained and chopped

Salt to taste

Thinking about packing a picnic? Give this simple recipe to your sweetie and fill your picnic basket with fresh fruit, deli ham and cheese, a bottle of wine, a book of poetry (try *American Primitive* by Mary Oliver), a blanket, and all those extras that make a day in the park a day to be remembered.

YIELDS 2 TO 3 SERVINGS

Bring a large pot of salted water to boil over high heat. Boil the potatoes for 10 to 15 minutes, or until tender; drain.

While the potatoes are cooking, boil the egg and cook the bacon. To hard-boil the egg, place the egg in a small saucepan and fill with cold water to cover by 1 inch. Set over high heat. When the water comes to a boil, start timing, and simmer the egg for 10 minutes. Remove the egg and place in an ice bath. When cooled, peel and chop. For the bacon, set a large skillet over medium heat and cook until crisp. Drain on paper towels and then chop into small pieces.

Combine the mayonnaise, vinegar, lemon juice, Dijon, dill, lemon thyme, and pepper in a large bowl. Stir in the bacon and onion. Fold in the egg, artichokes, and potatoes, combining gently. Taste for salt, and add more if needed. Serve warm or cover and chill for at least 1 hour and up to 24 hours.

artichoke pizza
with feta and thyme

hummus-like purée makes this pizza unique

For my friends and me, pizza has become our staple of choice for rented movies. Popcorn when you pay; pizza when you rent. Pick the right movie (*Lost in Translation or Bull Durham*, perhaps?), the right person, and most certainly, you'll see that you have a pizza that can take things to the next level.

YIELDS 2 TO 3 SERVINGS

Preheat the oven to 450 degrees. Add the olive oil to a medium skillet set over medium-high heat. Add the bell pepper rings and sauté for 3 minutes, or until just tender. Reduce the heat to medium and add the garlic. Cook another 1 to 2 minutes, or until fragrant but not browned.

Combine the mayonnaise, crushed red pepper, black pepper, and artichoke hearts in a food processor. Process until finely chopped.

Place the pizza crust on a baking sheet. Spread the artichoke mixture evenly over the crust and top with the bell pepper rings and garlic. Sprinkle with the cheeses and thyme. Bake for about 15 minutes, or until the cheeses are melted and bubbly.

1   teaspoon olive oil

1   small red bell pepper, sliced into thin rings

½   small yellow or orange bell pepper, sliced into thin rings

2   cloves garlic, crushed

¼   cup mayonnaise

¼   teaspoon crushed red pepper flakes

⅛   teaspoon freshly ground black pepper

1   (9-ounce) can artichoke hearts, drained

1   (12-inch) pre-made pizza crust

½   cup crumbled feta cheese (2 ounces)

½   cup freshly grated Parmesan cheese

½   teaspoon dried thyme

steamed artichoke leaves with green goddess dressing

yes, he loves me

2   artichokes

⅓   cup sour cream

½   tablespoon Champagne
    vinegar

⅓   cup mayonnaise

3   tablespoons buttermilk

    Salt and freshly ground
    black pepper to taste

    Zest of half a lemon

1   tablespoon chopped
    fresh tarragon

½   tablespoon minced chives

1   teaspoon minced parsley

Eating steamed artichoke leaves is a lot like playing that childhood game of "He loves me, he loves me not . . .," where you pluck the petals from a daisy until you know the Truth. Only with this game, you get to lick the creamy Green Goddess dressing off the leaves when he loves you, and scrape the tender flesh with your sharp teeth when he loves you not.

YIELDS 2 SERVINGS

Trim off the stem so that the artichoke will sit flat on a plate. Snap off the really tough outer leaves around the base, if you like. Trim off the top third of each artichoke with a sharp knife. Wash the artichokes well, spreading the leaves slightly so the water can run through. Turn upside down and shake well.

Place the artichokes in a large, microwave-safe bowl and fill with about 1 inch of water. Cover and microwave about 6 to 8 minutes, and then let sit for another 10 minutes, still covered. Pull out a leaf. Taste it. If it pulls out easily and tastes soft, then it's done. If not, microwave the artichokes for a few more minutes.

While the artichokes are steaming, prepare the green goddess dressing. Combine all the ingredients in a small bowl. Cover and chill until ready to use.

Place the steamed artichokes on a plate or in a bowl. Hot, room temperature, or chilled artichokes — all will taste divine. Spread apart the center leaves and fill with the green goddess dressing. Or, if you prefer, simply serve the dressing on the side. Eat, leaf by leaf, with your partner.

sicilian bruschetta with artichokes and olives

unbelievable flavors

For someone who has never prepared an artichoke, the task can seem quite daunting. But don't let it be. Here are the basics: Store the artichoke in a plastic bag in the coldest part of the refrigerator. Don't cut an artichoke until you're ready to use it. It will turn brown almost immediately. (Rubbing cut surfaces with lemon juice or storing the cut artichoke in lemon water helps stop discoloration.) To get to the heart of the artichoke, cut off the stem. Snap off the really tough outer leaves. Here's where my instructions differ from most other cookbooks, which tell you to slice off the top third of the artichoke, snip off the thorns, scrape out the choke – which is near impossible before you cook it – and then boil or steam for 45 minutes. Make your life easier: Skip all those steps and pop that artichoke in the microwave. Place in a bowl with about 1 inch of water. Cover and microwave about 6 to 8 minutes, and then let sit for another 10 minutes. Pull out a leaf. Taste it. If it pulls out easily and tastes soft, then it's done. If not, microwave it for a few more minutes. To get to the heart, pluck off all the leaves, and refrigerate until ready to eat at your leisure. (Dip the leaves in the Green Goddess Dressing on the previous page or go for the fool-proof standby, melted butter.) Pull the now easy-to-remove choke off with your fingers, and you're left with a beautiful artichoke base.

YIELDS 2 TO 3 SERVINGS

Set a large sauté pan over medium-high heat and add the oil. Sauté the sliced garlic, salt, pepper, and artichokes until the artichokes are tender enough to mash. (Add 1/4 cup to 1/2 cup of water, cover, and continue to cook if the artichokes aren't tender enough.)

Mash the artichoke mixture in the skillet with a fork. Stir in the olives, tomato, parsley, and capers to the pan. Toast the bread and rub with the remaining clove of garlic. Drizzle with the remaining olive oil. Spoon with the artichoke mixture and garnish with fresh parsley.

- 1½ tablespoons olive oil, plus more for drizzling
- 2 cloves garlic, thinly sliced, plus 1 clove for seasoning
- Salt and freshly ground black pepper to taste
- 2 medium artichoke hearts, chopped
- 5 oil-cured ripe olives, pitted and chopped
- 1 small tomato, seeded and chopped
- 2 tablespoons chopped fresh Italian parsley, plus additional leaves for garnish
- 1 tablespoon capers
- 2 thick slices French or Italian bread

g i n g e r

Its invigorating scent, sharp flavor, and medicinal qualities have made ginger a bona fide aphrodisiac for a millennia • Ginger root is actually the underground, spreading stems of the ginger plant. It works its way through the earth, forming a large bundle of twists and turns. Small portions of these twists and turns are called "hands," and that's what we buy today in the grocery as fresh ginger. • Eaten straight, it tastes zippy and hot on the tongue. Cooked, it transforms into a more subtle, spicy-sweet flavor. Mixed with sugar in a ginger chew, it provides a sticky, intense nectar for the tongue. Cold ginger ale bubbles down, soothing the stomach. Hot-from-the-oven gingerbread, eaten in days of yore by European maidens in the hopes that their gingerbread man would turn into a real husband, fills any kitchen with warmth. • Beyond the senses, ginger helps with a myriad of medical issues, calming motion sickness, alleviating migraines, and thinning the blood. The last of these issues plays the strongest role in ginger's aphrodisiac qualities by allowing blood to flow easily to all parts of our system, engorging the body's most sensitive areas with oxygen-rich blood. And we all know what that means.

grilled grapefruit
with ginger-mint syrup

a marriage of sour, spicy, and sweet

1   cup granulated sugar

1   cup water

1   (3-inch) piece fresh ginger,
    peeled and coarsely sliced

3   large sprigs fresh mint, plus
    more for garnish

1   large pink grapefruit

According to Kimberly and Mike in Memphis, Tennessee, "This recipe is a fantastic metaphor for great sex – something explosive with juices squirting everywhere – the senses go wild!" On a tamer note, the tart grapefruit combined with the minty-sweet syrup makes for a refreshing end to a rich meal, cleansing the palate for whatever the next course may be.

YIELDS 2 SERVINGS

For the syrup, combine the sugar and water in a small saucepan over medium heat, stirring until the sugar is completely dissolved. Add the ginger and let steep for 10 minutes to infuse the syrup. Add the mint sprigs, turn off the heat, and let steep 10 more minutes. Taste the syrup. If it's well infused with the flavors of ginger and mint, strain the mixture into a jar and refrigerate for up to 5 days, or until ready to use. If it needs more flavor, return to a low heat and continue to steep until the desired taste is reached.

For the grapefruit, set a grill pan over high heat. Slice the grapefruit in half along the equator. Using a sharp knife, make slits on both sides of each membrane to release the fruit from the pith. Brush the flesh with the ginger-mint syrup. Place, flesh-side down, on the hot grill pan. Let cook 5 minutes, or until well-caramelized grill marks appear.

To serve, cut around the inside perimeter of the fruit to completely release the flesh from the peel. Spoon with more ginger-mint syrup to taste and garnish with fresh mint.

roasted pumpkin
and ginger soup

madeira adds sweetness, devon cream decadence

This easy-to-make soup will get you feeling very cozy on a brisk autumn evening. The recipe calls for fresh pumpkin or squash; if you prefer, you may substitute a pound of canned pumpkin or frozen butternut squash, but in that case limit the simmering time to 7 minutes.

"Not big fans of nuts, Jessie and I decided to skip the walnuts and add some fresh sage leaves from the window box. We didn't have any clotted cream on hand, so we used plain yogurt for a bit of tang and added mouthfeel. We wrapped ourselves in thin wool blankets, poured our warm soup into big mugs, and sat together on our front steps in the cool night air, drinking in the autumn flavors of our soup."

Tim and Jessie, together 2 years, Denver, CO

YIELDS 2 OR 3 SERVINGS

Preheat the oven to 400 degrees. Spread the walnuts on a rimmed baking sheet, and toast until lightly browned, about 7 minutes. Set aside.

Place the pumpkin and apples in a large saucepan and add enough stock to cover. Stir in the ginger and bring to a boil over high heat. Reduce the heat to low and simmer until the pumpkin is tender, about 30 minutes.

Use an immersion blender to purée the soup. Or, working in batches if necessary, transfer the soup to a blender and purée. (If you're using an especially powerful blender, definitely work in small batches, as the steam released by too much hot soup may cause the blender's lid to blow off!) Return the puréed soup to the saucepan and add the cream in a thin stream, whisking as you do so. Add the salt and pepper and stir.

Spoon a dollop of Devon cream into each soup bowl, and drizzle 1 or 2 teaspoons of Madeira on top. Pour the soup into the bowls and garnish each with some toasted walnuts.

½ cup walnuts, coarsely chopped

1 pound peeled pumpkin or butternut squash, cut into 1-inch cubes

1 Delicious or other sweet apple, peeled, cored, and cut into slices

2 to 2½ cups chicken stock

2 teaspoons finely grated fresh ginger

¼ cup heavy cream

Salt and freshly ground black pepper to taste

Devon or clotted cream

Madeira or amontillado sherry

grilled vietnamese gingered beef rolls

for the filling:

- ½ pound ground beef, not extra lean
- ½ pound ground pork
- 4 cloves garlic, minced
- 2 teaspoons nuoc cham (Vietnamese chile sauce)
- 2 tablespoons soy sauce
- 1 tablespoon sesame oil
- 2 teaspoons minced fresh ginger
- ½ cup chopped fresh cilantro
- ½ teaspoon sugar
- Freshly ground black pepper to taste
- ¼ cup minced green onions
- ¼ cup grated carrots
- 24 canned grape leaves, rinsed well of brine

for the dipping sauce:

- 1 teaspoon fish sauce, or more to taste
- ½ cup water
- 2 tablespoons rice wine vinegar
- 2 teaspoons sugar
- ¾ teaspoon crushed red pepper flakes
- 2 cloves garlic, minced
- 3 tablespoons grated fresh ginger
- 2 tablespoons grated carrots
- 2 teaspoons chopped fresh cilantro leaves
- 2 teaspoons chopped green onions

These rolls are like little presents wrapped in grape leaves. There's no way to eat them but with your fingers. If your partner even considers using a fork and knife, pop him on the hand, preferably with a little crop. That's red. With a set of suede hearts for the Cat O'Nine Tails. Tell him he's been a bad, bad boy, and then make him watch you eat them all by yourself.

YIELDS 4 TO 6 SERVINGS

To prepare the filling, place all the ingredients in a large mixing bowl. Using clean hands, combine all the ingredients quickly and gently, being careful not to overwork the meat, or it will toughen. Place a grape leaf flat on a clean work surface. Place a heaping tablespoon of the meat mixture on the grape leaf. Fold the sides over, and roll the leaf up snugly to enclose the stuffing.

For the dipping sauce, combine all the ingredients in a mixing bowl. Divide among little serving cups. For a quicker go, pick up some dumpling sauce at your favorite Asian restaurant.

Prepare a hot grill. If using wooden skewers, soak in water for 30 minutes before grilling to keep them from burning. Set 2 skewers parallel and thread 1 grape roll crosswise onto the 2 skewers. This will keep it from unrolling. Add 3 to 4 more grape rolls onto each set of skewers. (Alternatively, skip the skewers and cook the rolls in a grill basket.) Grill over a hot fire for 6 minutes per side, or until slightly charred and just cooked through. Alternatively, cook under the broiler, turning once, until just cooked through. (The rolls become dry if overcooked.) Serve immediately with the dipping sauce.

honey ice cream with ginger-spiced pecans

sweet just got sweeter—and smoother

Watching an automatic ice-cream maker do its work can be just as hypnotizing as staring at a blazing fireplace – and a lot more interesting on the level of anticipatory thrill. (When the fire burns out, all you've got is a heap of ashes; when the ice-cream maker's done, you've got a luscious dessert.) This honey ice cream is "pure" – that is, unadulterated by any other sweeteners or flavors save those of the milk, cream, and egg yolks. The glazed pecans heighten the dish's honey sweetness – and add a nutty crunch and a prick of gingery spice to boot.

YIELDS ABOUT 1 1/2 QUARTS

To make the ice cream, combine the milk and honey in a small saucepan and heat over medium-high heat until the honey begins to melt and dissolve, 1 to 2 minutes. Remove the pan from the heat and stir until the honey is completely dissolved. Do not allow this mixture to boil, as it will curdle.

In a medium-size mixing bowl, whisk the egg yolks together with the salt for 30 seconds, then gradually whisk in the hot milk-and-honey mixture. Return the mixture to the saucepan and cook over low heat, stirring constantly, until the mixture coats the back of a spoon. Again, do not allow it to boil, or it will curdle.

Pour the hot mixture through a strainer into a medium-size bowl, add the cream and half-and-half, and let cool to room temperature. Cover with plastic wrap, and then put the bowl in the refrigerator and chill until very cold, 2 to 3 hours. Freeze in an ice-cream maker according to the manufacturer's instructions.

While the ice-cream maker is doing its work, make the glazed pecans. Preheat the oven to 300 degrees. Line a rimmed baking sheet with parchment paper or a silicone baking mat. Whisk the egg white in a small bowl until foamy. Add the honey and whisk to blend. Add the ginger and salt and combine well. Add the pecans, stir to coat, and spread the nuts in a single layer on the prepared baking sheet. Bake for 30 to 35 minutes, stirring every 10 minutes, until the nuts are a rich caramel color. Let cool and transfer to a storage container or serving dish so they don't fuse to the parchment. Add a handful of glazed pecans to each dish of ice cream just before serving.

for the ice cream:

- 1   cup whole milk
- 2/3 cup honey
- 4   large egg yolks
- 1/8 teaspoon kosher salt
- 3/4 cup heavy cream
- 3/4 cup half-and-half

for the glazed pecans:

- 1   large egg white
- 2   tablespoons honey
- 1/2 teaspoon finely grated fresh ginger
- 1/4 teaspoon kosher salt
- 6   ounces (about 1 1/2 cups) pecan halves

spicy gingered shrimp

finger-licking good

Juice and zest of 2 limes, plus 1 lime cut into wedges for garnish

3 hot chile peppers, seeded and sliced

1 stalk lemon grass, outer leaves discarded and interior stalk thinly sliced

1 (2-inch) piece ginger, grated (about 2 tablespoons)

2 cloves of garlic, crushed

2 tablespoons honey

⅓ cup olive oil

1 tablespoon chopped cilantro, plus more for garnish

1 pound jumbo shrimp (16/20 count), deveined and shelled, if desired

Salt and freshly ground black pepper to taste

"I'll remember feeding him the spicy flavored shrimp – his tongue trailing my saucy fingers so slowly that I'm positive time stopped. I'll remember him rubbing the spices along my mouth, only to lick them off seconds later. I'll remember lips on fingers, tongues on mouths, heat and honey. And I will never think of grilled shrimp the same way again." *Anne, on her experience with spicy grilled shrimp and Eric, 6 dates in 2 weeks, Jacksonville, FL*

YIELDS 2 TO 3 SERVINGS

If using wooden skewers, soak them in water for 30 minutes to prevent them from catching fire on the grill. Combine the lime juice, zest, chiles, lemon grass, ginger, garlic, honey, olive oil, and cilantro in a casserole dish large enough to accommodate the skewers; mix well.

Thread 4 shrimp on 2 parallel skewers to keep them from spinning on the skewers. Repeat with the remaining shrimp. Add the skewers to the marinade, turning several times to coat well. (As an alternative to skewers, marinate the loose shrimp in a large, resealable plastic bag. Grill in a grill pan instead of skewering.) Refrigerate 30 minutes to I hour at the most, turning once or twice while marinating.

Prepare a grill with a medium-hot fire or preheat the broiler. Remove the shrimp from the marinade. Season with salt and pepper. Grill or broil for 2 to 3 minutes per side, or until just cooked through. Garnish with additional cilantro and lime wedges.

avocado boats with baby shrimp and ginger sauce

luscious flavor combination

This is a fine way to deck out a ripe avocado. The sauce melds beautifully with the avocado's buttery flavor, and the pink shrimp make an enticing color counterpoint to the avocado's luscious green.

YIELDS 2 SERVINGS

Preheat the oven to 400 degrees. Spread the sesame seeds on a rimmed baking sheet and toast until lightly browned, 3 to 4 minutes. Set aside.

In a small bowl, combine the soy sauce, water, vinegar, sesame oil, garlic, scallions, ginger, and brown sugar. Let stand at room temperature until ready to serve.

Steam the shrimp in a sieve or strainer over simmering water until just heated through, about 10 minutes. Do not overcook.

Cut the avocado in half and remove the pit. Carefully scoop out the avocado half with a spoon, being careful to keep the avocado intact. Place each half on a salad plate. Divide the warm shrimp and arrange in and around the avocado halves. Drizzle each with sauce and lightly sprinkle with sesame seeds. Serve immediately.

1/2 teaspoon white sesame seeds

1 tablespoon soy sauce

1 tablespoon water

1 1/2 teaspoons rice wine vinegar

1 teaspoon sesame oil

1 medium-size clove garlic, crushed and minced

1 1/2 teaspoons finely sliced scallion (white and green parts)

1/2 teaspoon finely grated fresh ginger

1/2 teaspoon brown sugar

3/4 cup small (90 count) fully cooked frozen shrimp

1 ripe Haas avocado

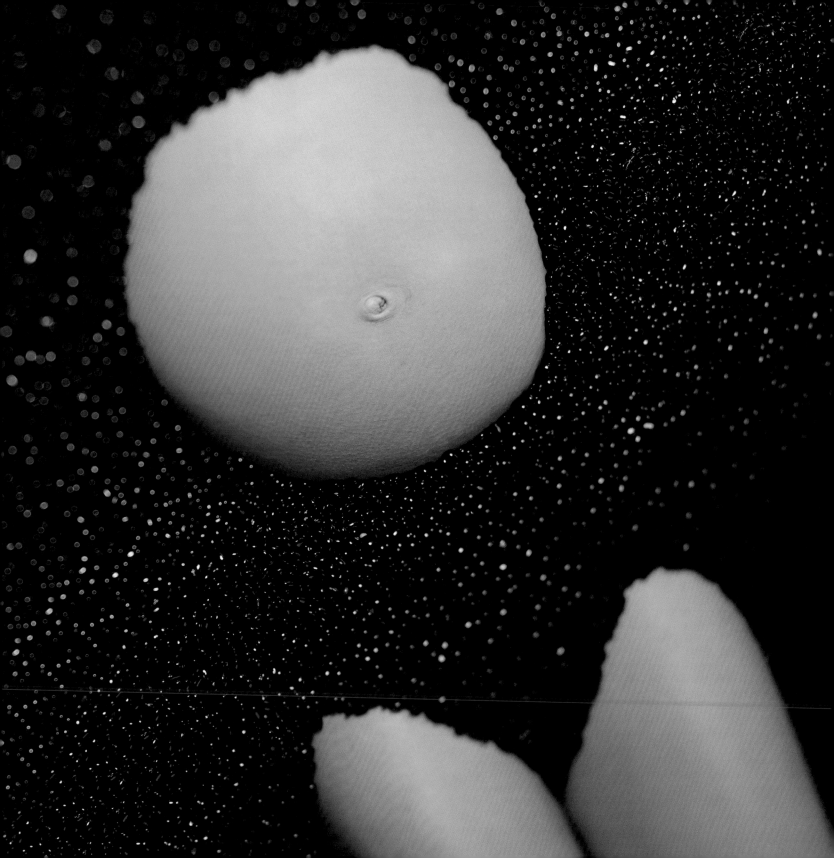

black beans

It was around 400 A.D. when Saint Jerome, a Father of the Latin Church, first told his nuns "No." No, that is, to black beans. No touching, no eating, no puréeing, no refrying them. Well, perhaps his edict was not that restricting. But he did get his point across — for a nun avowed to celibacy, black beans were bad news.

• Lore has it that they increase fertility: It all starts with the fresh bean pod. Nestled in its protective casing, the black bean rests like a child in its mother. Then, when it is time, it emerges a smooth, blue-black color of midnight. Cleansed in water, it turns a magnificently shiny black, smooth like a pebble washed down from years of wear. Once cooked, the bean becomes a plump, yet firm symbol of a woman with child. And so the cycle continues, creating love and children everywhere.

sweet bean pudding

exotic breakfast or dessert option

1 cup black beans, in their juice

1 teaspoon grated orange zest

1/3 cup plus 1 tablespoon
 sugar, divided

1 (14-ounce) can coconut milk

2 tablespoons water
 Pinch of salt

3/4 cup short-grain white,
 Jasmine, or Arborio rice

1/2 teaspoon vanilla extract

2 banana leaves
 (or 4 tamale husks)

1 ripe banana, cut lengthwise
 and then in half

A dear friend of mine lost her first baby during her eighth month of pregnancy. After two years of trying, she finally conceived again. In her eighth month of pregnancy, she agreed to pose for the black bean image, to symbolize its aphrodisiac quality of fertility and healing for women. On June 12, 1996, she gave birth to the most beautiful baby boy the world has ever seen. He weighed 8 pounds, 12 ounces, and he's just as sweet as this sweet bean pudding. [*Update: When* InterCourses *first came out, Davis Kidd Booksellers in Memphis hosted a book signing for us. Being a hometown crowd, several news crews and hundreds of people showed up. So did baby bean, who signed books with a thumbprint on the picture of his mother's belly. He's now an active fifth grader who plays baseball and performs in school plays. "When he grows up, he wants to be either a major league baseball player, an actor, or a chef," his mother says. "He'll probably end up working at McDonald's," she adds with a smile.*]

YIELDS 5 SERVINGS

Mash the beans with the orange zest and 1 tablespoon of the sugar in a small bowl. Combine the remaining 1/3 cup of sugar, the coconut milk, water, and salt in a medium saucepan set over medium-high heat. Bring to a boil. Add the rice. Bring back to a boil, and then reduce the heat to medium-low. Cook, stirring frequently, for 12 minutes, or until the milk is absorbed and the rice is just al dente. Remove from the heat, stir in the vanilla, and allow to cool.

Fit a large pot with a steamer basket and fill with enough water to come just to the basket. Set over high heat and bring to a boil. Cut the banana leaves into 5 x 7-inch rectangles and place horizontally on a work surface. On each rectangle, spoon 1 tablespoon of rice in a small, rectangular shape in the center of the leaf. Spoon 2 tablespoons of the beans on top of the rice. Set one-fourth of the banana on the beans, and then top with another tablespoon of rice. Fold the bottom half of the leaf up, fold in the two sides, and then fold over the top to make a little packet. If the leaf is brittle and has split, wrap snugly in foil to keep the contents from seeping out.

Add the packets to the steamer rack over the boiling water, adding more water if needed during the cooking. Steam, covered, for 45 minutes, or until warmed through. Let cool slightly to handle. Remove the foil and serve in the banana-leaf packets, as you would homemade tamales.

black bean chili

for wintertime warmth

As with all great chilis of the world, this one is better on day two. Don't flinch at the abundance of onions and garlic. While not officially covered in this cookbook, they are both well-regarded aphrodisiacs according to many. And besides, if both of you smell like garlic and onions, then who will be bothered?

YIELDS 2 TO 3 SERVINGS

Pick through the beans and remove any shriveled pieces or rocks. Place the beans in a large bowl and cover with water. Let soak overnight.

The next day, drain and rinse the soaked beans. Place the beans in a large stockpot set over high heat. Add 3 cups of water and bring to a boil. Skim and discard any foam given off by the beans. Add the red pepper, onion, celery, tomatoes, carrot, garlic, vinegar, beer, cayenne, and chiles to the beans. Simmer, covered, for 1½ hours, or until the beans are tender.

While the beans are cooking, brown the ground chuck and chorizo in a skillet set over medium-high heat. Add the salt, and season with pepper to taste. Drain well to remove any grease and add the meat to the beans. Cover and simmer for another hour for the flavors to meld. Taste and adjust the seasonings if needed.

To serve, ladle the chili into bowls and garnish with green onions, cilantro, Cheddar, and a dollop of sour cream. Serve with tortilla chips for a bit of crunch.

1   cup dried black beans,
    soaked overnight

3   cups water

1   small red bell pepper
    or ½ a medium, chopped

1   medium onion, chopped

1   rib celery, chopped

1   (14½-ounce) can diced
    tomatoes

1   medium carrot, grated or
    finely chopped

3   cloves garlic, minced

2   tablespoons white
    wine vinegar

½   cup beer

½   teaspoon cayenne pepper

2   tablespoons chile powder,
    or more to taste

½   pound ground chuck

½   pound chorizo sausage,
    casings removed

1   tablespoon salt,
    or more to taste

    Freshly ground black pepper
    to taste

for garnish:

    Chopped green onions

    Chopped fresh cilantro

    Grated Cheddar cheese

    Sour cream

    Tortilla chips

black bean salsa

capitalizes on the best produce of mexico

1   *ripe mango, peeled and diced*

¼   *red bell pepper, diced*

¼   *green bell pepper, diced*

¼   *red onion, diced*

½   *cup canned black beans, drained and rinsed*

⅓   *cup pineapple juice*

    Juice of 2 limes

¼   *cup chopped cilantro*

1   *tablespoon ground cumin*

½   *tablespoon minced green chile pepper*

    Salt and freshly ground black pepper to taste

Carlene and Turner, together 50 years as of March 1997 and parents of an unbelievable daughter named Martha, describe this salsa as "a very satisfying dish with a definite exotic flavor."

I never like to hear of my parents' love life. (Parents, as we all know, do not have sex. Especially ones who were missionaries for 10 years. No gratuitous sexual puns, please.) But the following description was tame enough to keep me from wincing. Says Carlene, "It brought to mind Caribbean beaches and a romantic dinner for two under the swaying palm trees. This added romantic excitement to the evening." My father reinforced her quote with a grin and a wink. *[Update: My parents still do not have sex. Never have; never will – grins and winks not withstanding. How they ended up with 4 children, 8 grandchildren, and 3 great grandchildren will always remain a mystery.]*

YIELDS 2 TO 3 SERVINGS

Combine the mango, peppers, onion, black beans, juices, cilantro, cumin, and chile pepper in a bowl. Season with salt and pepper. Chill, covered, for up to 2 days. Serve as a snack with tortilla chips or, better yet, fried plantain rounds.

"He made me a margarita, fluffed up my favorite chair, put on some Ruben Blades, and brought over a bowl of black bean salsa and chips.

That's why I love him."

Amy, on her husband Steve, who still, after 11 years of marriage, manages to surprise her with his kind heart, Tupelo, MS

black bean fritters

meltingly good

Grapeseed or peanut oil
for frying

½ cup cornmeal

½ cup flour

½ tablespoon baking powder

1 tablespoon packed
brown sugar

Salt and freshly ground
black pepper to taste

½ red bell pepper, diced

½ yellow bell pepper, diced

½ chayote or zucchini, diced

1 cup cooked black beans

1 large egg, beaten

2 tablespoons buttermilk

I first made this dish for a co-ed bridal shower/bon voyage gift to a co-worker who would be traveling to Greece with her fiancé and three-carat diamond for a wedding on the beach in Cyros. All in attendance oohed and ahhed over these fritters drizzled in an almost-drinkable vinaigrette, and the couple is still married. Must be the beans. *[Update: The couple is still happily married and, rumor is, they're living on a beach in the Keys à la Jimmy Buffet.]*

YIELDS 2 TO 3 SERVINGS

Set a large saucepan over medium-high heat and fill with enough oil to come halfway up the sides.

Combine the cornmeal, flour, baking powder, brown sugar, salt, and pepper in a large bowl. Add the bell peppers, chayote, and black beans. Toss lightly with your hands to coat. Pour in the egg and buttermilk, and toss just to combine.

When the oil reaches about 350 degrees and sizzles when you add a drop of batter, drop the black bean mixture into the oil by large spoonfuls. Golf-ball size fritters work best. Fry 3 to 5 minutes, or until thoroughly warmed through and crispy. Serve with the tropical vinaigrette.

1 mango, peeled and
seeded (the mango seed:
another fun play toy for
couples)

½ cup passion fruit juice or
pomegranate juice

Salt to taste

Honey to taste

½ cup rice wine vinegar

3 tablespoons freshly
squeezed lime juice

2 tablespoons orange juice

1 cup peanut oil or olive oil

tropical vinaigrette

smooth and delicious

This recipe creates more than enough vinaigrette for the fritters. But by all means, do not throw the leftover away. Save and serve later over fruit salad, grilled chicken, or, god forbid, iceberg lettuce.

YIELDS 2 TO 3 CUPS

Blend the mango, passion fruit juice, salt, and honey in a blender. With the blender running, drizzle in the vinegar, lime juice, orange juice, and then peanut oil. Store, refrigerated, in an airtight container until ready to use. Shake well before using.

mango-black bean empanadas

pequeños pockets of yumminess

"I've experienced the sun's descent over Montjuïc in Spain. I've been caressed by the evening winds of the Gulf of Mexico in San Pedro. But never has the night moved in Memphis like it did over these empanadas. Tasty black beans simmering with spices and cilantro make the senses scream, "Vamanos!" A minor amount of prep work opens the door for interludes as your partner tangos past you for this or that ingredient, quick to grab you instead of the skillet. Sampling the black beans in progress gives your partner a taste of the evening to come: spice and heat, with a teaser of fruit, leaving you miles away from ordinary. Served underneath Mexican party lights in your location of choice, these empanadas are a tantalizing treat for the senses and tribute to summer nights as they draw to a close. It makes you hug your man and start hummin' a song from 1962 . . . ain't it funny how the night moves?" *"B" and Jay, together 18 years, Memphis, TN*

Victoria and Keifel, married five years and living in Nashville, TN, took an aphrodisiac detour with the mango salsa: "In our house, cutting up a mango is always an excuse for deliciously inappropriate behavior. We love the tempting, heady scent of a ripe mango. There is nothing like licking sticky mango juice off fingers, or faces, sucking the seed over the sink, so as not to waste any mango flesh, mind you." They enjoyed the empanadas as well.

YIELDS 9 EMPANADAS

1 tablespoon olive oil
¾ cup finely diced yellow onion
1 (15-ounce) can black beans, undrained
1 tablespoon ground cumin
¼ teaspoon cayenne pepper
Splash of beer or water for moistening, if needed
¼ cup chopped fresh cilantro
Salt and freshly ground black pepper to taste
Butter for greasing
1 (17.3-ounce) package frozen puff pastry (2 sheets), thawed
1 ripe mango, peeled and diced, or 3 tablespoons mango chutney
1 large egg, beaten

Set a heavy, medium-sized skillet over medium heat and add the oil. Sauté the onion until translucent. Stir in the beans, cumin, and cayenne; cook until the mixture is hot, about 5 minutes. Add a splash of beer or water if needed to keep from drying out. Stir in the cilantro, and season with salt and pepper to taste. Using a potato masher or the back of a fork, mash the bean filling to a very coarse paste and let cool.

Preheat the oven to 425 degrees and grease a rimmed baking sheet. Roll out each puff pastry sheet on a lightly floured surface to a 14-inch square. Cut each sheet into 9 squares with a sharp knife. Place 1 heaping tablespoon of filling in the center of each square. Divide the diced mango evenly among the filled squares or spoon with 1 teaspoon of the chutney. Brush the inside edges of the squares with the beaten egg. Fold on the diagonal over the filling to form a triangle. Using the tines of a fork, seal the crust edges well. Arrange on the baking sheet and brush the tops with the remaining egg. Bake until golden brown, about 15 minutes. Serve hot.

black bean shepherd's pie with corn pudding

a marriage of cheese, chorizo, beans, and corn

3/4 pound Mexican chorizo

Butter for greasing

2 cups milk

1/2 cup stone-ground white
cornmeal

4 ears corn, husked, and
kernels cut from the cob,
or 1 to 2 (12-ounce) cans
corn, drained

1 teaspoon salt, plus more
to taste

2 tablespoons sugar

3 tablespoons unsalted butter

1/2 teaspoon freshly
grated nutmeg

4 large eggs, separated

1/4 cup diced roasted red pepper

1 (15 1/2-ounce) can black
beans, drained

Freshly ground black
pepper to taste

1 1/2 cups shredded Monterey
Jack cheese

"I was trying desperately to get into the spirit of the black beans, but was finding it a bit difficult because of my very pregnant state. It's ironic I got this recipe now – I should have tried it five years ago when I was first trying to get pregnant. Oh well. But to help out a friend who is trying to get pregnant, I invited her and her husband over for dinner to black bean their way into fertility. Fingers crossed.

We ate the shepherd's pie, and everyone really liked it – not a bite left among the four of us. But on the aphrodisiac front, I felt stuffed, tired, and ready to go to bed with no energy for play. Luckily, Kirk was on the same page, and we both fell asleep. That's when my unexpected aphrodisiac experience happened: I had a great sexual dream about Kirk, my husband of nine years and the father of our upcoming baby. Frankly, any sexual dream that I've had in the past usually involved someone totally unattainable: Dennis Quaid, Colin Firth, my high school boyfriend. And pregnancy hasn't enhanced any aphrodisiac experiences for me. Just the opposite, in fact. So it was a welcome dream, to say the least, and plenty of deep, subconscious aphrodisiac for me." *Allison, mother-to-be and wife of Kirk, Waco, TX*

YIELDS 4 SERVINGS

Sauté the chorizo over medium-high heat until browned thoroughly, stirring and breaking up the ground meat as it cooks. Drain any excess grease from the chorizo. Preheat the oven to 350 degrees and butter a casserole dish with high sides or a standard 8 x 8 x 2-inch dish. For an intimate alternative, make individual servings in ramekins.

To make the corn pudding, set a large saucepan over medium heat, add the milk, and bring to a simmer. Increase the heat to medium-high and slowly stir in the cornmeal. Let simmer for 5 minutes, stirring constantly so the cornmeal doesn't burn. Transfer to a large bowl and let cool for 15 minutes. Add the corn, salt, sugar, butter, nutmeg, egg yolks, and bell peppers to the cooled mixture, stirring well to combine. Whisk the egg whites in a separate bowl until they are light and fluffy and form soft peaks. Fold into the mixture a little at a time until incorporated. (continued)

Spread an even layer of the black beans in the bottom of the casserole dish. Season with salt and pepper to taste. Distribute the cooked chorizo on top of the beans, and then sprinkle with the shredded cheese. Carefully spread the cornmeal mixture on top of the cheese in an even layer. Bake for 30 to 45 minutes, or until the topping has browned and seems firm. Don't open the oven door while cooking, as that may deflate the soufflé-like fluffiness of the corn pudding. If it deflates, don't worry — it will still taste wonderful. Remove from the oven and let rest at least 5 minutes to allow the layers to set. Cut into squares or scoop out with a spoon to serve.

baby bok choy
with black bean sauce

good-for-you never tasted so good

Baby bok choy are the immature heads – four or five inches long, with white stems and dark green leaves – of the vegetable also known as Chinese cabbage. This ultra-easy stir-fry recipe calls for fermented black beans. Sold in Asian groceries, fermented black beans (also called "dried black beans") have the slightly spongy texture of dried fruit and generally come packaged in plastic bags.

Y I E L D S   2   S E R V I N G S

Wash the bok choy thoroughly, pinching off any flowers and trimming any uneven stem-ends. In a large saucepan, bring 1 quart water to a boil. Add 1 tablespoon vegetable oil and the pinch of baking soda to the water, stirring to dissolve the soda. Add the bok choy and cook until the green leaves brighten, about 30 seconds. Immediately remove the pan from the stove and drain in a colander, spraying the bok choy with cold water to stop the cooking.

Heat a wok or large sauté pan over high heat until very hot. (A drop of water splashed into the wok should evaporate immediately.) Add the remaining 2 tablespoons vegetable oil and swirl, heating for an additional 30 seconds. Add the black beans, garlic, and ginger and sizzle — stirring vigorously — for 15 seconds. Add the bok choy and stir to coat. Sprinkle in the salt and sugar and continue to stir, very energetically, for 2 to 2½ minutes. Add the sesame oil, stir once more, and serve immediately.

3/4 pound baby bok choy

3 tablespoons vegetable oil, divided

Pinch of baking soda

2 teaspoons fermented (or "dried") black beans

1 large clove garlic, very finely minced

1 quarter-size slice fresh ginger, peeled and very finely minced

1/2 teaspoon salt

1/2 teaspoon sugar

1/2 teaspoon sesame oil

oysters

Perhaps the greatest of all aphrodisiacs, the oyster symbolizes virility and passion for all who indulge. From Petronius to Casanova, oysters have unleashed their powers of seduction on unwitting prey and restored life to lagging libidos. • The oyster's powers are best experienced when eaten on the half shell. In this state, the oyster looks fresh, jiggly, meaty, and wet. For some, it represents the masculine with its similarities to the testes. But for most, it is the feminine exposed, naked, resting in its half shell, nether petals of pink and gray fluttering out from the meat onto a pearly white backdrop. • If the sheer visual effects of the oyster do not suffice, add in their briny flavor, salty like the sea, their smooth, slip-down-your-throat texture, and their substantial nutritional benefits to the human body. • They are low in fat and high in complex sugars and proteins. More importantly, though, oysters are loaded with zinc, a key ingredient to testosterone production and sexual performance for both genders.

oysters on the half shell

the quintessential staple of aphrodisiac foods

1 cup high-quality ketchup

¼ cup horseradish sauce

Juice of 2 lemons

Dash of Tabasco

Oysters on the half shell, as many as your heart desires

Shucking can be fun (with protective gloves and an oyster knife, that is). First, scrub and rinse the oysters thoroughly in cold water to prevent grit from invading the succulent morsel you're working so hard to get to. Next, work the knife into the slit near the "hinge" of the shell. Twist the knife forcefully until the shell begins to pop open. Work the knife around the rest of the shell to open completely. Detach the oyster from the shell so it'll slide easily into your mouth.

YIELDS 2 SERVINGS

To make a basic cocktail sauce, combine the ketchup, horseradish, lemon juice, and Tabasco. Serve as a side to oysters on the half shell.

curried oysters with chardonnay

delicate bites of oyster coated in warm cream

24 oysters on the half shell

1 tablespoon unsalted butter

2 shallots, minced

1 cup Chardonnay or other dry white wine

1 cup heavy cream

1 teaspoon Madras curry

Salt and freshly ground black pepper to taste

"Making this dish reminded us of our honeymoon 29 years ago in Cape Cod. We ate tons of oysters in many different dishes on that beautiful paradise by the ocean. What oysters did for us then, they still do for us today (maybe it's just the memories). Whatever the case, we believe it is romance in the form of food. Use wisely, and only with those who deserve it." *Matt and Carol, married 29 years, Philadelphia, PA*

YIELDS 2 SERVINGS

Preheat the oven to 450 degrees. Drain the oysters, reserving the juice. Set a sauté pan over medium heat. Add the butter and sauté the shallot for 2 to 3 minutes to soften. Add the wine and reserved oyster liquor. Bring to a boil. Reduce the heat and simmer for 6 to 8 minutes, or until the liquid is reduced by half. Strain into a saucepan, discarding any solids.

Stir in the cream to the saucepan and bring to a boil. Reduce the heat and simmer for 10 to 12 minutes, or until the liquid is reduced again by half. (For a thicker sauce, dissolve 1 tablespoon of cornstarch in 2 tablespoons cold water to make a slurry. Add bit by bit to the sauce until slightly thickened.) Add the curry and salt to the sauce.

Arrange the oysters (in their shells) in a roasting pan. Season each oyster with pepper and top with a tablespoon of sauce. Bake for 3 to 4 minutes, or until the oysters are just cooked and the cream is beginning to brown.

victuals and rituals

Food is Brahman (God), the Hindu declares,
and I have often thought it so. Neither *halal* nor *haram*,
but Nature's bounty all, everything
kosher . . .
       O *taste and see*
Not apples, pomegranates, and bananas (Fruits of Knowledge though they be)
But the twilight realm of *transubstantiation*, where the body lies

suspended

somewhere between yearning and actuality. And bread and wine
host the difference
       between what is
       and what might be.
Everything *pasand* . . .
       O *taste and see*
The raw materials from which the soul is made.
Wondrously
Divine.

Darren J. N. Middleton

After they had swallowed a few oysters and drank one or two glasses of punch, which they liked amazingly, I begged Emilie to give me an oyster with her lips . . . I placed the shell on the edge of her lips, and after a good deal of laughing, she sucked in the oyster, which she held between her lips. I instantly recovered it by placing my lips on hers . . . My agreeable surprise may be imagined when I heard her say that it was my turn to hold the oysters. It is needless to say that I acquitted myself of the duty with much delight . . . [later] I scolded Armelline for having swallowed the liquid as I was taking the oyster from her lips. I agreed that it was very hard to avoid doing so, but offered to (show) them how it could be done by placing the tongue in the way. This gave me an opportunity of teaching them the game of tongues, which I shall not explain because it is well known to all true lovers . . . It so chanced that a fine oyster slipped from its shell as I was placing it between Emilie's lips. It fell onto her breast, and she would have recovered it with her fingers; but I claimed the right of regaining it myself. I got hold of the oyster with my lips, but did so in such a manner to prevent her suspecting that I had taken any extraordinary pleasure in the act. Casanova, Memoirs, Volume 6, Translated by Vera Lee in Secrets of Venus

parmesan cheese oysters

the jalapeños just keep things hot

Jeffrey, who loves to vacation in the Pacific Northwest for veritable oyster orgies with his girlfriend, believes that "oysters supersize a pedestrian moment; they intensify it." He continues, "Oysters bathe a regular dinner in an enchantment not otherwise possible. I just love them – they're sensual and aesthetic, they're briny, they're the sea. Eating them brings real pleasure. Wait, this is beginning to sound pretty autoerotic. Well, uh, I guess it is."

YIELDS 8 OYSTERS

Preheat the oven to 450 degrees. Cook the pancetta in a large skillet set over medium heat until crisp. Drain and chop into small pieces, reserving the grease in the pan. Add the onion, bell pepper, and jalapeños to the skillet and cook just until the onion and peppers soften.

Combine the pancetta, onions, peppers, Parmesan cheese, butter, and breadcrumbs in a small bowl to form a thick paste. Arrange the oysters (in their shells) on a baking sheet. Spoon the mixture evenly among the oysters. Bake for 10 minutes, or until the oysters are just cooked through and the breadcrumbs are golden brown.

- 3 to 4 slices pancetta or bacon
- ¼ cup chopped onion (about ½ small onion)
- ¼ cup chopped red bell pepper (about ½ small pepper)
- 2 jalapeños, seeded and diced
- ¼ cup freshly grated Parmesan cheese
- 4 tablespoons unsalted butter, softened
- ½ cup seasoned bread crumbs or panko
- 8 shucked oysters, on the half shell

cheddar cheese oysters

artichoke hearts add another layer of flavor

YIELDS 8 OYSTERS

Preheat the oven to 450 degrees. Combine the artichokes, Cheddar cheese, butter, and breadcrumbs in a small bowl. Arrange the oysters (in their shells) on a baking sheet. Spoon the mixture evenly among the oysters. Bake for 10 minutes, or until the oysters are just cooked through and the breadcrumbs are golden brown and the cheese is melted and bubbly.

- ¼ cup chopped artichoke hearts
- ¼ cup shredded Cheddar cheese (about ⅛ pound)
- 2 tablespoons unsalted butter, softened
- ¼ cup seasoned bread crumbs or panko
- 8 shucked oysters, on the half shell

blue cheese oysters

the pungent cheese intensifies these oysters

YIELDS 8 OYSTERS

Preheat the oven to 450 degrees. Combine the blue cheese, garlic, breadcrumbs, and butter in a small bowl. Spoon the mixture evenly among the oysters. Bake for 10 minutes, or until the oysters are just cooked through and the breadcrumbs are golden brown and the cheese is beginning to melt.

- ½ cup crumbled blue cheese
- 1 teaspoon chopped garlic
- ¼ cup seasoned breadcrumbs
- 2 tablespoons unsalted butter, softened
- 8 shucked oysters, on the half shell

malpeque oysters with thai chile mignonette

the best of the ocean's bounty

2 tablespoons sesame oil

2 tablespoons grapeseed oil

1 tablespoon chopped
fresh ginger

½ teaspoon minced garlic

½ teaspoon minced red
Thai chile

2 tablespoons thinly
sliced green onions

2 tablespoons Champagne
vinegar, or more to taste

Pinch of sea salt

12 fresh Malpeque oysters,
scrubbed clean

J.C. didn't know what a ruckus he would create with this recipe. J.C., that's Chef de Cuisine Jean-Charles Dupoire of Epic Restaurant in the Fairmont Royal York in cosmopolitan Toronto, Canada, if you want to get specific. We hosted a week-long aphrodisiac extravaganza one Valentine's holiday. We fed the guests multiple courses of aphrodisiacs, lowered their inhibitions through copious rounds of libations, and then sent them upstairs to their beautifully apportioned rooms to let fate have its way with them. When J.C. first made these oysters in our aphrodisiac cooking class, you could see the couples eyeing their partners over the shells as they slurped down the ice-cold oyster, senses sent into shock from the taste of the mignonette. They listened politely for the remainder of the class, but J.C. knew, and I knew, they did not care. The oysters had taken over. Our field tests showed more of the same.

YIELDS 4 SERVINGS

For the mignonette, combine the sesame oil, grapeseed oil, ginger, garlic, and Thai chile in a medium saucepan set over low heat. Let infuse for 10 minutes to extract the flavors. Remove from the heat and let cool to room temperature. After cooling, add the green onion and vinegar.

To serve, place crushed ice or rock salt on 4 cold plates to stabilize the oysters. Shuck the oysters, being careful not to lose their flavorful liquor. Arrange 3 oysters on each plate, and spoon some of the mignonette sauce over each oyster. Serve immediately. (continued)

malpeque oyster field test results

together 9 minutes

"How could I have even known that going to check out a title problem could be so fun? Instead of the 50-something lawyer I expected to meet, voilà Kris, and suddenly legal issues became much more interesting. For about 30 minutes we studiously reviewed the title and then, to my (and perhaps his?) surprise, we spent the next hour sharing our own stories. What started in that conference room continued a short time later at his place with pinot, oysters, and chiles in tow. While I started the spicy mignonette, he valiantly wrestled with the un-shucked oysters, wrenching each of them open with a victorious 'Ha!' and dashing grin. Although our oysters turned out to be a partial disaster (not all were as fresh as we would have hoped in our land-locked city) it only added extra flavor to our evening full of laughter and stories. Here's to unexpected delights." *Heather and Kris, first date, Austin, TX*

together 9 months

"I was a little worried about oysters, because, quite frankly, I'm not a huge fan. But, how can you resist it when the most beautiful woman you know says, 'Really? You don't like them? I dunno, oysters make me horny!' But the Thai sauce added just the right spice, blending with the salty ocean flavor of the oysters to make something more than palatable, but actually good. Eden wasn't lying. Oysters do work on her, and me too." *Greg, Eden's catch-of-the-day, San Luis Obispo, CA*

   "I've always known what oysters can do to me, and that's why I was excited to try this recipe. I'm glad to report that, not only do I love the little mollusk morsels, but the Thai chile sauce made them the best I've ever had. Don't be afraid to let the juices run everywhere . . . like I said, that little bit of chile adds a special spice wherever it lands." *Eden, Greg's saucy little oyster, San Luis Obispo, CA*

together 9 years

"Heather doesn't eat raw oysters, so this recipe is absolutely perfect for the ol' hot/cold. I seared scallops in a small amount of olive oil, and then she served me the cold oysters with the mignonette and I poured the mignonette over the seared scallops, among other things . . . Perfect, really. Isn't it all about pleasing each other? Sure didn't taste like a compromise." *Rob and Heather, Salinas, CA*

fried oyster salad
with rémoulade dressing

sexy, succulent morsels

for the rémoulade dressing:

½ cup mayonnaise

1 tablespoon coarse-ground mustard

1 tablespoon minced shallot

1 clove garlic, minced

2 teaspoons capers

1 teaspoon Worcestershire sauce

Tabasco to taste

⅛ teaspoon anchovy paste

Salt and freshly ground black pepper to taste

1 teaspoon Champagne vinegar

Milk or buttermilk, if needed

for the oysters:

Grapeseed oil for frying

12 to 16 fresh oysters (about 1 cup shucked)

Salt and freshly ground black pepper to taste

Tabasco to taste

½ cup cornmeal

3 tablespoons flour

2 pinches cayenne pepper, or more to taste

for the salad:

1 bag organic field greens, washed and spun dry

2 lemons, quartered

"The last time Ted shucked oysters was at a friend's house over the holidays. Men and women cooed by his side, amazed at his strength, like he was the only man on the planet who knew his way around a bivalve. Remembering that, I was tempted to buy fresh Fanny Bays, but in a time crunch, I bought a jar filled with huge, almost fist-size beasts. I wanted to cut them into smaller pieces; he wanted to bite into the full-figured meats. We opted for big pieces, to keep the sexy bellies intact, so we had something juicy to taste. Mixing the slippery oysters with my hands was the first turn-on. The second: watching him fry them up in a pan." *Lesley and Ted, 10 years and counting, Pasadena, CA*

"I impressed my new, voluptuous squeeze with the ease of preparation. 'Very savoir faire,' she remarked. Being also from the South, she digs fried oysters, which are something not quite so approachable to folks from other regions. I added extra Tabasco, and that's what really got her going, so much so that I got lucky after quite a long dry spell. The secret is: don't over-fry the oysters. They should be sensual and mushy inside." *Caleb and Joann, still too early to tell, Los Angeles, CA*

YIELDS 2 MAIN COURSE SERVINGS OR 4 APPETIZERS

For the rémoulade dressing, combine all the ingredients in a small mixing bowl. Taste and add more Tabasco, salt, and pepper as needed. If the dressing seems too thick, add a bit of milk until the desired consistency is reached. Cover and chill until ready to use.

For the oysters, preheat the oven to 200 degrees to keep the finished oysters warm. Fill a large, heavy saucepan with enough oil to come halfway up the sides. Warm over medium-high heat to 350 degrees, or until a flicker of flour sizzles when it hits the grease. Cut each oyster in half or thirds for manageable bites. Season with salt, pepper, and Tabasco. Mix with your hands to distribute the seasonings. Combine the cornmeal and flour in a shallow bowl. Season with more salt and pepper, and add the cayenne. Stir to combine. Dredge each oyster piece in the cornmeal mixture and set into the hot oil. Cook 2 to 3 minutes, or until perfectly crispy on the outside. Drain on paper towels. Keep warm in the oven on a wire rack set over a baking sheet until ready to use. (continued)

To assemble the salad, place the lettuce in a large mixing bowl and add several tablespoons of dressing. Gently toss with your hands to coat the leaves. Add more dressing as needed, but do not over-dress. Place a large handful of leaves on each salad plate, scatter with the fried oysters, and garnish with fresh lemon wedges. Serve any extra dressing on the side.

grilled oysters

the next best alternative to raw

Oyster aficionados Marie and Richard tested this recipe, reaffirming in the process the oysters' aphrodisiac powers over them: "Oysters take us back to our honeymoon in New Orleans, when we consumed three or four dozen a day. Perhaps that memory contributed to the fun we had now, three years later, grilling oysters together and eating them in our make-do, candle-lit picnic in the living room floor." *[Update: Marie and Richard have, sadly, divorced, but they both still carry a strong torch for oysters. Marie's new husband won't touch the things. Richard's girlfriend enjoys them, though not as much as he. At the end of the day, marriages are rarely 100 percent good or 100 percent bad. With the distance of time and the relief of lives less intertwined, it's sometimes easier to understand both the good and bad of a former partner. The years spent together don't feel in vain, and you can appreciate the good things, the good times, you shared. So it goes with the oysters for these two, when eating them together brought moments of contentment and happiness, even in the midst of sometimes less-happy days.]*

1 dozen oysters in the shell, scrubbed clean

3/4 cup breadcrumbs

3 tablespoons finely chopped fresh parsley

1 clove garlic, crushed

Juice of 1/2 lemon

2 tablespoons olive oil, or more to taste

Salt and freshly ground black pepper to taste

YIELDS 2 SERVINGS

Prepare a medium-hot grill. Remove the top shell of the oysters, being careful to not lose any of their liquor. (It will make a nice juice for the oysters to simmer in.)

Combine the breadcrumbs, parsley, and garlic in a small bowl. Spoon on each oyster. In the same bowl, combine the lemon juice, olive oil, salt, and pepper. Drizzle over the oysters. Grill for 12 minutes, or until the breadcrumbs are golden. Alternatively, place under a broiler just until the oyster liquor begins to bubble and the breadcrumbs begin to brown.

For an even simpler version, simply clean the oysters, place on medium-hot grill, and remove when they begin to open. Shuck, squeeze with lemon, et voilà.

r o s e m a r y

Unmistakable. The scent of rosemary fills a room, distracting you from the mundane smells of life. Whether growing in a sunlit window planter, flavoring olive oil and hot country bread, or scenting the soft curve of a woman's neck, rosemary seduces with its aroma. • Madame de Sévigné found rosemary intoxicating. Medieval women allured men with their rosemary-scented bath water. Perfumeries have incorporated its captivating smell into many a formula. • You can use the herb to play on humans' keen "scent memory" — our "strongest tie to most emotional experiences," according to Cynthia Watson in *Love Potions*. As the theory goes, if the scent of rosemary is present during a particularly amorous event, the smell of rosemary will always be associated with the same good feelings you experienced as a couple, transporting you back to the intimate moment when you first smelled the piney herb together. If executed properly, one may eventually evoke a Pavlovian "call to love" with a mere waft of it in the air. • Rosemary's charm extends well beyond its fragrance, with a woodsy taste of pine and tactile properties appropriate for rooms beyond the kitchen. The soft needles on a sprig of rosemary tickle every nerve ending they brush past.

crisped rosemary chicken

no napkins allowed

1 brick

2 chicken breasts, with skin, or 2 chicken thigh-leg pieces, with skin

Salt and freshly ground black pepper to taste

2 cloves garlic, thinly sliced

1 tablespoon chopped fresh rosemary

1 tablespoon olive oil

Here's the truth: I hate chicken breasts. Really, tell me, why do they exist? They're as flavorless as they are ubiquitous. But one day, I experienced chicken breasts anew. I was helping host a culinary tour of LA that included a prix-fix lunch at Campanile. (Scarlett Johansson was dining in the back, and yes, she's as beautiful in person as one would hope, an aphrodisiac incarnate for both genders.) Our large group had two choices — a chicken breast or something else equally uninteresting. I chose the chicken, expecting something way less than stellar. Oh me of little faith! Glory be to God! That was the best chicken to ever pass my lips. And it was breast meat, no less! If you don't have the time or money to get hot-and-bothered in person at Campanile for their Crisp Flattened Chicken with Beurre Fondue or any other divine thing on their menu, here's my humble rendition of Chicken Under a Brick, simplified for us non-LA folk.

"Because Asher has cooked chicken for me in celebratory times throughout our relationship, it already had sentimental, sexy connotations. This particular recipe was simple but good, and we lit candles and drank wine to heighten the mood. Dinner lasted a good hour, with great conversation flowing."
Danielle and Asher, together 3 years, Brooklyn, NY

"Juicy, salty, crispy, and delicious." *Brian and Maggie, together 10 years, Seattle, WA*

YIELDS 2 SERVINGS

Find a brick from your garden or garage. Brush off any critters. Wrap the brick well in aluminum foil. Set a cast-iron skillet over medium heat. While the skillet is heating, rinse the chicken and pat very dry. Set the chicken pieces on a clean work surface and push back the skin, but do not remove. Season the meat with salt and pepper. Place the garlic slivers and most of the chopped rosemary on the meat, and then pull the skin back down to cover the meat. Drizzle the skin with the olive oil and rub to distribute evenly. Season with more salt and pepper to taste, and sprinkle with the remaining rosemary.

When the skillet is warmed through — but not so hot as to burn the skin quickly — place the chicken, skin-side down, in the pan and top with the brick or another heavy skillet. Cook 10 to 15 minutes, until the skin is a glorious, crispy treat, and then turn to finish cooking. (Once the chicken is flipped, you do not have to top it with the brick, though you may.) Continue cooking until a thermometer registers 165 degrees and the juices run clear. If the skin is cooking too fast, finish the chicken off in a 350 degree oven until safely cooked through. Serve with risotto or mashed potatoes and a crisp green salad.

rosemary-scented lamb over pasta

satisfyingly rich

During my summer in Paris, I met a Lebanese man named Kamal. Toward the end of my stay, he invited me over for dinner. Being the naive 19-year-old that I was, I met him at his house for an eight o'clock dinner. A complete gentleman the whole evening, he showed me around his cracker-box apartment and told me about his life as an officer in the Lebanese army. He showed me pictures of his palatial estate in Lebanon. And then he showed the after-pictures of rubble, the war scars on his back, and the letters from family he had to leave behind. He made me lamb and pasta that night; we ate in his kitchen on a make-shift table with daisies he'd picked from his window box. I never saw him again. *[Update: At the time of this revision, there is continued turmoil in Lebanon. Beirut, it is said, has been destroyed and rebuilt seven times. Here's a good-luck charm against the probable eighth, and to the couples on all sides who try, daily, to maintain a semblance of normalcy and love amidst the destruction and chaos of war.]*

YIELDS 2 TO 3 SERVINGS

½ pound rigatoni, cooked

3 tablespoons olive oil, divided

2 cloves garlic, thinly sliced

½ yellow or red bell pepper, cut into strips

6 ounces lamb, cut into thin strips

Salt and freshly ground black pepper to taste

½ cup dry white wine or chicken stock

1½ cups crushed tomatoes

Sprig of fresh rosemary

¼ cup heavy cream

1 teaspoon finely chopped fresh rosemary

1 teaspoon chopped fresh sage

1 teaspoon chopped fresh oregano or ½ teaspoon dried

¼ cup freshly grated Parmesan cheese

Bring a large pot of salted water to boil. Cook the pasta according to the package instructions and drain, reserving 1 cup of pasta water to use if needed. While the pasta is cooking, set a large skillet over medium heat, and add 1½ tablespoons of the olive oil. Add the garlic and bell pepper and sauté until softened. Remove to a small plate.

Increase the heat to medium-high and add the remaining 1½ tablespoons of olive oil. Place the strips of lamb evenly in the hot skillet, being careful not to overlap them, and season with salt and pepper. Let cook for 2 to 3 minutes, or until browned. Turn each strip over, season with salt and pepper, and let cook until thoroughly browned on the other side. Remove to the plate with the garlic and bell pepper.

Increase the heat to high and pour the wine into the pan to deglaze, scraping the bottom with a wooden spoon to release any flavorful browned bits. When the wine has almost entirely reduced, add the tomatoes and the sprig of rosemary. Simmer for 15 minutes. Stir in the cream and the reserved lamb, bell peppers, and garlic. Add the warm rigatoni and the chopped rosemary, sage, and oregano; toss to coat with the sauce. If the sauce is too dry, add a bit of the reserved pasta water and cook until heated through and reduced to the desired consistency. Taste and add more salt and pepper if needed. Sprinkle with Parmesan, and serve immediately.

rosemary-bacon croquettes

our favorite treat on the back roads of spain

- 2 cups milk
- 2 sprigs fresh rosemary, plus 2 tablespoons minced
- 1 clove garlic, minced
- ½ cup olive oil
- ½ cup flour
- ½ teaspoon salt
- Freshly ground black pepper to taste
- Pinch of freshly grated nutmeg
- ½ pound bacon
- ½ cup shredded manchego cheese
- 1 cup fresh breadcrumbs or panko
- 1 large egg
- Vegetable oil for frying

Patience is a virtue, especially when it comes to these melt-in-your-mouth croquettes. So don't get whiny when you realize the béchamel needs to set up overnight. Just put the sauce in the fridge, think of another way to seduce her in the meantime, and dream of dancing croquettes in the Andalusian countryside to make the night pass quickly. You may want to plan on a bubble bath for post-croquette consumption. These crispy morsels tend to leave a glistening sheen on your chin . . . and everywhere else they've been.

"Frying up the bacon for this recipe, I was reminded of Mae West's famous line from *I'm No Angel*: 'When I'm good, I'm very good. But when I'm bad . . . I'm better.' There is absolutely nothing sexier than watching a committed vegetarian throw his morals to the wind and devour a strip of bacon. It is the ultimate indulgence: sweet, salty, smoky rich, and forbidden (if you're lucky). You may have a hard time convincing your partner to leave enough bacon for the croquettes, but do; they're worth it." *Gwyneth and a Naughty Vegetarian, Albuquerque, NM*

YIELDS 4 TO 6 SERVINGS

Set a large saucepan over medium-high heat and add the milk, rosemary sprigs, and garlic. Bring almost to a simmer, and then turn off the heat. Let steep while you make the roux.

Set a large sauté pan over medium heat and add the olive oil. To make a roux, whisk in the flour and let cook for 2 to 3 minutes, or until very light brown. Return the saucepan of milk to medium-low heat. Whisk in the roux, making sure to dissolve any lumps. Add the salt, pepper, and the nutmeg. Bring to a boil and cook for 5 minutes, or until the mixture is thick like pudding. Discard the rosemary sprigs, and pour the mixture into a storage container.

Let cool about 15 minutes, and then stir in the cooked bacon and shredded cheese. Cover and refrigerate overnight to let the béchamel set up.

The next day, set four bowls in a row, with a plate at the beginning and end of the row. Place a piece of waxed paper on each plate. In the first bowl, place the minced rosemary and season with salt and pepper to taste. In the second, pour in half of the breadcrumbs. In the third, add the egg and beat with a fork. In the fourth, add the remaining breadcrumbs.

Fill a large saucepan or Dutch oven with oil enough to come halfway up the sides and warm over medium-high heat until 350 degrees, or until a sprinkle of breadcrumbs sizzles when it hits the oil. Preheat the oven to 200 degrees to keep the finished croquettes warm. (continued)

Roll the refrigerated béchamel mixture into tiny bite-size balls and set on the first plate. Sprinkle the balls with the rosemary mixture, and then roll in the breadcrumbs. Dip the croquettes into the beaten egg, and then roll again in the breadcrumbs. Set on the last plate until ready to fry.

Fry the croquettes in batches for 3 to 5 minutes each, or until golden brown and warmed through. If not serving immediately, place on a wire rack set over a baking sheet, and keep warm in the oven.

capellini with rosemary

ideal use for ripe summer tomatoes

According to Dan of Sioux City, Iowa, "At the very least, this recipe made me look like I know how to cook. She got all impressed that I was using fresh herbs — whatever it takes, you know. I casually left some well-chosen poetry books next to the couch. (It's one of those chair-and-a-half couches. Another smart purchase on my part.) And while I have no definite proof of the correlation between rosemary and what happened later on, I am forever indebted to capellini with rosemary, Norton and his anthologies, and that too-small couch." *[Update: Neither Dan nor I have any clue whom he cooked this recipe for. This is not surprising, as Dan is a gypsy at heart. Now living in Austin, he is continuing to woo women with poetry and snug couches. These tactics always work because he's so loveable, so charming, and, ultimately, so unavailable.]*

YIELDS 2 TO 3 SERVINGS

Bring a large pot of salted water to a boil over high heat. Cook the pasta according to package directions until al dente.

While the pasta is boiling, combine the tomatoes with one-fourth of the garlic, 1 tablespoon of the olive oil, and the vinegar in a small bowl. Set a large skillet over medium heat and add the remaining ¼ cup of olive oil. Add the shallots and cook 3 to 4 minutes, or until they begin to soften. Stir in the remaining garlic and continue cooking until the garlic becomes fragrant and mellows slightly. Stir in the rosemary, parsley, and chives, and remove the pan from the heat. Toss with the hot, cooked pasta.

Place on a warmed serving dish and top with the tomato mixture. Serve immediately.

1 pound capellini

1 pound (about 3 medium) tomatoes, diced

4 cloves garlic, thinly sliced, divided

¼ cup plus 1 tablespoon olive oil, divided

1 tablespoon balsamic vinegar

2 shallots, minced

2 tablespoons very finely chopped fresh rosemary

¼ cup chopped fresh parsley

¼ cup chopped fresh chives

Salt and freshly ground black pepper to taste

herbed risotto

a chewy, delicately-scented dish

3 tablespoons unsalted butter

1 small onion, diced

1 tablespoon minced
  fresh rosemary

5 cups chicken stock

1 pound cremini mushrooms,
  sliced

¾ cup Arborio rice

¼ cup white wine

¼ cup heavy cream

  Salt and freshly ground
  black pepper

⅛ cup chopped fresh basil

1 tablespoon freshly grated
  Parmesan cheese

1 large ripe tomato, seeded
  and diced

This risotto reminds me of my first experience with the creamy wonder: It was a late-night dinner following *City of Angels*. My date and I had wandered down one too many dark alleys when we stumbled upon a five-table trattoria nestled between two closed shops. The only thing they had left to serve was their Thursday special – mushroom risotto. Try this recipe with some wine, bread, and candlelight. It worked for us.

YIELDS 4 SERVINGS

Set a large, heavy saucepan over medium-high heat. Add 1 tablespoon butter, and then sauté the onion and rosemary until the onion is translucent.

In another saucepan, heat the chicken stock on medium-high.

Set another skillet over high heat and add 1 tablespoon butter. Sauté the mushrooms until they have released all their water and have started to brown. Add the sautéed onion and rosemary to the pan of sautéed mushrooms and set aside.

In the saucepan where you originally cooked the onion, add the final tablespoon of butter and stir in the rice. Cook over medium to medium-high heat, stirring frequently, until the rice becomes slightly translucent, about 7 to 10 minutes.

While the rice is sautéeing, microwave the white wine to warm. Add the hot wine to the rice. Stir until absorbed. Add the hot stock in ladlefuls to the rice, stirring frequently. Before all the liquid is completely absorbed, add another ladleful. Continue doing this until the rice is just barely al dente. (You may not use all of the stock. Be careful not to overcook the risotto — It should be a bit firm on the inside and creamy on the outside.)

As you're nearing the end of the stock, microwave the cream to warm. Stir in the warm cream, and season with salt and pepper to taste. Gently stir in the basil, Parmesan, tomato, onion, and mushrooms. Cover and let rest for 2 to 3 minutes for the cream to be absorbed. Serve immediately.

FRESH ROSEMARY IS NOT SOMETHING THAT I NORMALLY INCLUDE ON MY GROCERY LISTS. HONESTLY, I DIDN'T EVEN KNOW WHERE TO FIND IT. SO WHEN I BEGAN CHOPPING UP THIS HERB AND ITS PINEY SCENT FILLED MY KITCHEN SPACE, I WAS SLIGHTLY AMAZED. ITS PRICKLY NEEDLES SMELLED SO WARM AND OUTDOORSY. LIKE BEN.

BEN IS ALL LEATHER AND FLANNEL. ALL ROBERT REDFORD AND PAUL BUNYAN. ALL-FOR-ONE AND ALL-AMERICAN.

AND ALTHOUGH YOU'D NEVER GET HIM TO ADMIT IT

– BEN IS TOTALLY *rosemary*.

Leanne's response to a dinner of *capellini with rosemary* and Ben, her beau of 2 years, Fayetteville, AR

rosemary-manchego scones

smear with european-style butter

3 cups self-rising flour, preferably Martha White, King Arthur, or White Lily

1 teaspoon salt

1 tablespoon freshly ground black pepper

½ cup finely chopped rosemary, or less if desired

1 tablespoon sugar

8 tablespoons (½ cup) lard, chilled

½ to 1½ cups grated manchego cheese, depending on how cheesy you like your scones

1 cup buttermilk

"I met Josh, a soldier in the Israeli Army, in a neighborhood restaurant a week before he was returning to the Israeli-Lebanon border. His pending departure for a war zone sparked an unexpected urgency in me, so I gave him my email and encouraged him to keep in touch.

"An hour later there was an email waiting for me, and I replied that we should have coffee before he left. 'Would love that,' he wrote. So we made tentative plans for the weekend.

"I thought a sunrise paddle would be the ideal outing and planned to make rosemary-manchego scones and coffee. But his family's emotional tumult about his quickening departure gave him little time for adventures, culinary or otherwise.

"I made the scones anyway. It had been a long work day, and baking relaxed me. Chopping rosemary always reminded me of Ben, my ex-boyfriend, whose earnestness and intensity reminded me of Josh.

"Ben loved the earthy smell of rosemary, which we would mix with everything – pasta carbonara, roasted potatoes, grilled chicken, scrambled eggs. He would have liked the rosemary-manchego scones. When we were first together, we traveled to Spain, and it felt like a honeymoon, we both agreed. We returned from our trip with an entire wheel of manchego, whose sultry, musky odor filled our apartment for weeks.

"The scones were done at 11:30 p.m. I placed one on a ceramic plate and slathered it with butter. Then I poured myself a glass of sherry and made a toast: to old loves, new loves, and Josh's safe return." *Wendy and Josh, still awaiting their first date, Vermont and Israel*

YIELDS 8 SCONES

Preheat the oven to 400 degrees and line a baking sheet with parchment paper.

Place the flour, salt, pepper, rosemary, and sugar in a food processor and pulse just to combine. Add the lard and pulse just until the mixture becomes the texture of coarse meal. Place the mixture into a large mixing bowl and add the cheese and buttermilk, stirring until just combined. Remove the mixture to a floured surface. Using your hands, quickly work the dough into a circle about 8 inches wide and ¼ inch high. Cut the circle into 8 wedges with a sharp knife, as if cutting a pizza. Place the wedges on the baking sheet and bake for 13 to 18 minutes, or until just barely golden brown. Be careful not to overcook, as the scones will harden.

The scones are best eaten immediately, split open with a thick smear of softened butter or as a mini-sandwich of Serrano ham, sliced manchego, and a touch of mayonnaise to bind it all together.

rosemary~cheese grits casserole

for grits lovers everywhere

For those of you who have never tried grits, now is the time. Unbeknownst to most, grits are basically ground-up dried kernels of corn – nothing to be afraid of at all. If your partner claims to hate grits, tell him it's polenta. If he doesn't like polenta, tell him it's an Italian tamale casserole.

Y I E L D S   2   T O   3   S E R V I N G S

Preheat the oven to 350 degrees. Grease a 13-inch oval casserole. Combine the tomato purée, tomatoes, garlic, and rosemary in a bowl. Layer the grits cakes, tomato mixture, and fontina, half at a time in the casserole dish. Top with the Parmesan cheese. Bake for 30 to 40 minutes, or until heated through and the Parmesan is crusty and golden brown.

Butter for greasing

3   cups tomato purée

2   cups diced fresh tomatoes

4   cloves garlic, crushed

2   tablespoons minced fresh rosemary

   Grits cakes (see recipe below)

12   ounces fontina or mozzarella, shredded

½   cup freshly grated Parmesan cheese

grits cakes

like fried polenta, only better

Y I E L D S   2   T O   3   S E R V I N G S

Grease two 8 x 8-inch baking dishes. Combine the grits and rosemary, and prepare according to package directions.

Combine 1 of the eggs and the cream in a small bowl; mix well. Add some hot grits to the egg mixture to temper the eggs, beating well with a wire whisk to incorporate. Stir the mixture back into the remaining grits and whisk together well. Pour the grits into the baking dishes, and refrigerate until firm.

In a large, nonstick sauté pan, pour in enough oil just to cover the bottom of the pan and set over medium-high heat. Carefully cut the firm grits into manageable squares in the baking dishes and remove the squares with a spatula. Beat the remaining egg with the 2 teaspoons of water in a shallow bowl. Place the cornmeal on a plate. Dip each wedge first in the egg mixture, and then in the cornmeal. Fry in the skillet until golden brown and crispy on both sides. Drain on paper towels and then proceed with the casserole. Or, serve them alone as a side to grilled or roasted meats.

1   cup instant grits (or stone-ground, slow-cooking grits for an even better flavor)

2   tablespoons very finely chopped fresh rosemary

2   large eggs, divided

2   tablespoons heavy cream

   Peanut oil for frying

2   teaspoons water

¼   cup cornmeal

rosemary roasted pork with potatoes

the slow oven does most of the work

1   (6-pound) boneless pork shoulder butt, sometimes called Boston butt

1¼ cups rosemary, minced, divided

Salt and freshly ground black pepper to taste

⅓ to ½ cup olive oil

1   head garlic, cloves peeled and sliced in half lengthwise

1   pound new red potatoes, scrubbed clean

"Our kitchen, and bedroom for that matter, had been lacking, well . . . spice. I slowly, slowly cooked the pork rump, doused with rosemary and garlic, and was delighted at the outcome. The food tasted great – very savory. Then I tasted the spices again – on my husband's lips – and it was is if his lips had been marinated slowly, slowly, just for me.

"After our meal, and what followed, my husband went to the fridge and brought me a bowl of sliced strawberries I had prepared earlier. That – the sweet strawberries and the even sweeter act of Daniel bringing them to me – made the evening complete." *Daniel and Ann, married 3 years, Waco, TX*

"As far as I'm concerned, eating utensils are optional. Imagine this: a soft blanket spread out over the living room floor, candles lit everywhere, you and your lover feeding each other warm, soft pork with rosemary-scented juices flowing down your arm, and mopping up your plate with the crispy potatoes. Eating with your fingers has always been the secret weapon in my aphrodisiac pantry – something about the texture of food in your hands and the inevitable licking of the fingers is undeniably sexy and seductive." *Kelly and Pat, together 3 years, Toronto, ON, Canada*

YIELDS 6 SERVINGS

Preheat the oven to 225 degrees. The pork butt may have a thick layer of fat across the top. If it seems excessive, trim away a bit, but be sure to leave at least a thin layer of fat across the top. The fat will melt as the pork cooks, basting the meat through the long cooking time.

Reserve ¼ cup rosemary for the potatoes. Combine the remaining rosemary with salt and pepper in a small bowl. Add a tablespoon or two of the olive oil to make a paste. Make deep slits in the pork with a sharp knife all over the meat. Stuff 1 garlic slice and a bit of the rosemary paste into each slit. Liberally season with salt and pepper, and massage the remaining rosemary paste all over the surface. It's best to prepare the pork for cooking a day in advance to allow the flavors to penetrate the meat. Place in a large, resealable plastic bag and refrigerate until ready to cook.

For a finished pork butt that's crispy on all sides, place the meat, fat-side up, on a wire rack set over a high-rimmed baking sheet. This will allow the hot air to circulate around the meat and create a crispy crust all over. What you have in crispiness, though, you'll lose in drippings. (continued)

For pork that's crispy on top with plenty of drippings left in the pan, simply place in a large Dutch oven. For even more drippings, cover the Dutch oven — just know that you'll lose out on all the crispiness, which is a decadence I don't think one should miss. Roast the pork for 5 to 7 hours, or until most of the collagen and fat have melted and the meat is completely tender and flavorful.

While the pork is roasting, prepare the potatoes. Cut into 1-inch cubes and place in cold water to keep them from turning brown until they're ready to roast. About 2 hours before the pork is finished cooking, line a baking sheet with nonstick aluminum foil. (This kitchen product actually works, and you'll never have to scrape roasted potatoes from the pan again.) Drain the potatoes from their soaking water and place on the aluminum foil. Drizzle on some olive oil or pork drippings — start with 3 tablespoons, but add more if you like. Season generously with salt and pepper. Sprinkle on the reserved rosemary. Toss the potatoes and seasonings with your hands and spread evenly over the foil. Add to the oven and roast with the pork. Bake 1 to 2 hours, turning occasionally. After removing the pork from the oven, taste the potatoes. If they're not done, increase the heat to 400 degrees and continue roasting for up to 30 minutes, until creamy on the inside and crispy and golden on the outside.

Because of the fatty nature of pork shoulder, there are lots of pockets of fat that remain in the meat. Cut a large piece of aluminum foil and set it underneath a cutting board so that at least 6 inches extend beyond both the left and right sides. Set a serving plate near the cutting board, and transfer the entire pork butt to the cutting board. Using a knife, remove any crispy good pieces and set on the serving plate. Begin shredding the meat with 2 forks. As you come across pieces of fat, scrape them off the meat and onto the foil. Place the perfect, rosemary-garlic pork on the serving plate. If you come across large pieces of roasted garlic, mash them with your fork and add them to the serving plate. Continue throughout the entire cut until you have a plate piled with perfect meat. Wrap up the aluminum foil of scraps and throw away.

If there are any drippings left in the pan, return the meat to the pan and stir to coat. Set on medium-low to keep warm if the potatoes aren't quite done. You will have plenty of leftovers if serving only two, but this meat is so flavorful, you won't mind a few nights of repeats.

rabbit in mustard sauce
à la colette

a seal-the-deal dish

2 *sprigs fresh thyme*

1 *sprig fresh rosemary, plus extra sprigs for garnish*

3 *sprigs Italian parsley*

1 *bay leaf*

1 *(3-pound) rabbit, cut in 7 or 8 pieces, or 3 pounds skinless chicken thighs*

   Salt and freshly ground black pepper

2 *tablespoons olive oil*

1 *cup dry white wine*

⅓ *cup Dijon mustard*

2 *cloves garlic, crushed*

¾ *cup heavy whipping cream*

This dish is a specialty of my boyfriend's charmante mother, Colette. By now, she knows that it's the first thing I hope to taste the minute we make it to France. I could swim in the sauce it's so good, and I have been known to lick my plate at the table. Très gauche, I know. If you don't enjoy rabbit, chicken thighs will work equally well. But if you're avoiding the rabbit only because you're anxious about how it will taste, I encourage you to give it a try.

YIELDS 4 TO 6 SERVINGS

Prepare a bouquet garni by tying the thyme, rosemary, parsley, and bay leaf together with kitchen twine. Season the rabbit pieces with salt and pepper.

Set a large, heavy skillet or Dutch oven over medium heat. Add the olive oil and brown the rabbit pieces on all sides. To avoid over-crowding and steaming the meat, brown the pieces in batches. And take your time — to develop the flavor for the sauce, you want to create a flavorful brown fond (the drippings that stay in the pan). If you try to brown the pieces too quickly, the fond will blacken and your sauce will taste bitter.

Preheat the oven to 300 degrees. Remove the rabbit from the skillet; it will not be cooked through. Add the wine, increase the heat to medium-high, and scrape the bottom of the pan with a wooden spoon to deglaze and release the fond. While the wine is reducing, brush the browned rabbit pieces with mustard. Return the rabbit to the pan. Add the bouquet garni and garlic. Cover and place in the oven. Cook for 30 minutes, or until the rabbit is cooked through and the juices run clear.

Remove the rabbit from the pan and discard the bouquet garni. Return the pan to the stove top. Stir in the whipping cream, increase the heat to medium-high, and let simmer for 2 minutes. Check the seasoning and add more salt and pepper if needed. Return the rabbit to the skillet to coat with the sauce and warm through. Serve over rice or pasta or any sort of crusty bread to sop up the sauce. Garnish with fresh rosemary for a hint of green.

the story of coco and roro

a tale of culinary seduction

"Their fathers had been friends since childhood. After enlisting at 18, they lived through the horrors of World War I together. Afterward, they each married, started a family, and moved to different areas of France. Victor lived in the northeast, Pierre in the southeast. But their vacation houses were only 40 miles apart, so once a year the families tried to meet. By a strange coincidence, their last two children were born the same day of the same year, on November 2, 1936, one a girl, the other a boy.

"The two little ones grew up and became good-looking teenagers. A tender complicity grew between them. The young man, very athletic, did not fear bicycling 80 miles round trip over mountains and vales in a single day to visit the young woman. Mysteriously enough, the young woman always knew, though nobody knows how, when the young man would come. To thank him for his efforts and comfort him, she took the habit of preparing for him special dishes, including *lapin à la moutarde*, or tender rabbit bathed in mustard. Whether it was the young woman or the rabbit that seduced the young man is still unclear. Isn't love of good home cooking a powerful reason to go up and down mountains on a bicycle?

"For love of food or each other, the young woman and the young man got married and had three children. The most adventurous of all left to conquer America. There, he met the beautiful young woman who wrote this book, fell madly in love with her, and passed on to her the recipes of his mother and of his youth. *Translated from the French by Jean-François (better known as Jeff in these here parts), son of Colette and Robert*

flank steak with rosemary chimichurri

garlicky, drippy goodness

for the flank steak:

1 pound flank steak

2 tablespoons olive oil

   Salt and freshly ground
   black pepper to taste

for the chimichurri:

3 cloves garlic,
   coarsely chopped

1 teaspoon salt, plus more
   to taste

½ bunch fresh parsley, leaves
   removed and very coarsely
   chopped

½ bunch fresh cilantro, major
   stems discarded, remaining
   stems and leaves very
   coarsely chopped

1 sprig fresh rosemary,
   leaves removed and
   coarsely chopped

2 tablespoons freshly
   squeezed lime juice
   (about 1 lime)

   Freshly ground black
   pepper to taste

5 to 6 tablespoons
   extra-virgin olive oil

This particular chimichurri tastes more Latino with its heavy hit of cilantro and lime juice. For a more Italian approach, use parsley only and replace the lime with lemon or your favorite vinegar. You can make this dish with a food processor, but neither the texture nor the flavor compares to using a mortar and pestle. Do as you wish. But don't feel guilty if you choose the path of least resistance. As Lesley noted in her testing form, "The Cuisinart isn't sexy, but it sure is a time saver."

If the weather's pretty, escape the confines of the house for a picnic. Sandwich the ribbons of steak in a crusty bun, and pack it in a basket with a potato salad and those tiny bottles of sweet, fizzy wine. Take your lover down to a secluded spot and spread out a blanket. Eat the sandwich, drink the wine, and let the ambiance do the magic.

"My boyfriend is the proud grandson of a beef farmer, and he has fond memories of growing up on 'the farm,' especially the meals prepared with the loving and doting hands of his grandmother. Everything came from their own land: the peas they ate like candy, the baby beets, the carrots, the corn, and of course, their steaks and hamburgers. 'I remember the steaks and hamburgers,' he'll say. 'It was farm fare, but it was so good. I remember we had hamburger steak ground fresh from sirloin, with butter from the dairy down the road melting all over it.' His stories made me drool.

"Before I knew his stories, before I understood his nostalgic love for beef, the first meal I made him was a beef roast with rosemary and garlic, served with candlelight and plenty of red wine. It was what I did best. I still remember the way my tiny apartment smelled: the rich beef roasting with the savory rosemary wafting from my kitchen.

"It's three years later now, and we're both busy professionals. I have my own business, and he's running a small law firm. Neither of us have the time or energy to do a roast. But this steak makes our apartment smell the way it did that first night. *Kelly and Pat, together 3 years, Toronto, ON, Canada*

"I prep, he grills. That's how we do. The kitchen was heavy with herbal aromas arising from the chimichurri. When he walked by for a kiss, the smell of smoke and charred meat lingered on his hair. He kissed my fingers. Garlic. He stuck a sprig of rosemary behind my ear. We kissed again. The meat rested longer than five minutes. In fact, I think we got to it the next day." *Lesley and Ted, 10 years and counting, Pasadena, CA* (continued)

Remove the flank steak from the refrigerator and let come to room temperature.

To make the chimichurri, place the garlic and salt together in a large mortar. Grind and mash the garlic until it breaks down and begins to form a paste. Add the parsley, cilantro, and rosemary. Grind and mash the herbs with the garlic for a minute or so, and then add the lime juice and season with pepper. Continue grinding and breaking down the herbs. Pour in the olive oil, a little at a time, grinding and mashing in between each edition. Taste and adjust the seasonings as needed. The chimichurri may taste overly pungent on its own, but will add liveliness and flavor to the flank steak.

Alternatively, place all the ingredients in a food processor except for the olive oil. Process until well combined. With the motor running, drizzle in the olive oil until emulsified. Cover and refrigerate until ready to use.

To prepare the flank steak, set a grill pan over high heat or prepare a hot grill. Drizzle 1 tablespoon of olive oil on each side of the steak. Massage into the meat. Generously season with salt and pepper. When the pan is blazingly hot, cook the meat for 2 to 3 minutes per side for medium-rare, or until the desired degree of doneness. (Flank steak tastes wonderful when cooked from rare to just shy of medium. Beyond that, it moves into shoe leather range. Watch the doneness closely! If you have a piece that's thick at one end and thinner at the other, cut the slab into two pieces to better control the doneness.) Remove the meat to a plate and let rest 5 minutes. To serve, slice thinly on the bias, going against the grain. Drizzle the sliced steak with the chimichurri and serve immediately with warmed flour tortillas or grilled pita bread.

Refrigerate any extra chimichurri in an airtight container with a thin layer of extra-virgin olive oil over the top to help preserve it.

edible flowers

nasturtiums - fuchsia - lilies - hibiscus - roses - orange blossoms - jasmine - chrysanthemums
gladiolus - orchids - lilacs - lavender - marigolds - daisies - squash blossoms - violets - chamomile

"Flowers are the plants' sex organs, and they evoke the sex-drenched, bud-breaking free-for-all of spring and summer," says Diane Ackerman in A *Natural History of Love.* • Lore has it that the sweet juice of the honeysuckle induces erotic dreams. Jasmine has a musky, almost animal, scent that boosts feelings of well-being, passion, and joy. The hitch? It takes eight million blossoms to produce only one kilogram of the sensual oil. • Plucked off, one by one, daisy petals tell whether he loves me, or he loves me not.

A dandelion, with one swift puff of air, tells of a lover's faithfulness (or lack thereof) to a relationship. • As with people, beauty is in the eye of the beholder. Some light-up from the cheeriness of a Black-Eyed Susan, while others are seduced by the exquisite architecture of a single orchid. • Flowers speak when people can't: Red roses communicate love. A virginal white bud represents innocence and purity. A loose bouquet of wild-flowers speaks of carefree, happy love. Let the petals say whatever your heart desires.

floral wontons

crispy purses plump with sweetened cream cheese

1 bag hibiscus tea or
1 teaspoon loose tea

¼ cup hot water

4 ounces cream cheese,
softened

¼ cup edible flower petals,
plus more for garnish

3 tablespoons sugar, divided

24 wonton wrappers

Vegetable oil for frying

These treats have some of the same textures and flavors of that Chinese appetizer mainstay, crab rangoon. We've replaced the sweet crab meat with sweetened floral tea, transforming these crispy/creamy morsels into the perfect dessert-in-bed for you and your little flower.

YIELDS 24 WONTONS

Steep the tea in the hot water for 5 minutes, or until well infused. Combine the cream cheese, flower petals, 2 teaspoons of steeped tea, and 1 tablespoon of the sugar in a medium bowl. Mix well to combine.

Place ½ teaspoon of the cream cheese mixture into the center of a wonton wrapper. Lightly brush the edges with cold water. Cup the wonton in the palm of your hand and bring the 4 corners upward together to the center to make a little wonton purse. Place the stuffed wontons in the refrigerator while the oil is heating. (The wontons can be prepared to this point a day in advance, covered tightly, and refrigerated. They also freeze well. Place on a waxed-paper-lined baking sheet in a single layer and freeze. When frozen, transfer to a resealable plastic bag and freeze. When ready to use, place them again in a single layer on a baking sheet and thaw for several hours in the refrigerator before frying.)

Preheat the oven to 200 degrees to keep the finished wontons warm. Fill a large saucepan or Dutch oven with enough oil to come halfway up the sides and set over medium-high heat to 350 degrees. Drop an extra wonton skin into the oil. If it starts to sizzle immediately, the oil is ready. When hot, place 3 or 4 stuffed wontons in the oil and fry until golden brown. Drain on paper towels and keep warm on a wire rack set in the oven. Repeat until all the wontons are fried.

In a small bowl, combine the remaining 2 tablespoon of sugar with a few drops of the tea for coloring and flavor. (For a gooier, stickier solution, use honey in lieu of the sugar.) Sprinkle the sugar on the serving plate, place the warm wontons on the sugar, garnish with some petals, and serve immediately.

lemony kefta
with israeli couscous

baby meatballs scented with saffron

"The kefta was part of an aphrodisiac-testing marathon turned food orgy. Incredible flavor. We both love lamb, and we used one large serving spoon to feed each other." *Rob and Heather, Salinas, CA*

"My boyfriend and I love garlic and spicy things, so we doubled or tripled the cayenne and hot peppers, and threw in half a bulb of garlic, as well. We renamed it "Fidelity Kefta," since no one else would want to kiss us. Sexy? Maybe not very. But awfully romantic for meatballs." *Erik and Sophie, together 6 years, New York, NY*

This is one of those recipes where the smell permeates your kitchen, your home, your pores. You don't notice it so much while it's cooking. But then you run out to the car to get the datebook you left in the back seat, and you come back in the door and – wham! – it smacks you right in the face and then swirls around you and lures you into the kitchen for just one bite because you know that the scent of the lemon and saffron, the sound of the bubbling stock, the texture of the plump pearly couscous, the sight of the meatballs bobbing, you know it's all too much, and you can't wait for all this to turn into reality, into a first bite that makes you moan like you're having sex that feels so good your neighbors can hear. That's what these meatballs can do. Have fun.

YIELDS 4 SERVINGS

1	pound finely ground lamb
	Pinch of cayenne pepper, or more to taste
1	teaspoon ground cumin
1½	teaspoons ground cinnamon
3	large white onions, grated, divided
1	medium bunch Italian parsley, leaves chopped, divided
1	cup Israeli, or pearl, couscous
½	tablespoon extra-virgin olive oil, or more if needed
3	tablespoons unsalted butter
1	tablespoon minced fresh ginger
1	hot chile pepper, seeded and minced
	Pinch of saffron threads
1	small bunch cilantro (optional), minced
1	tablespoon freshly squeezed lemon juice
1½	cups water
	Salt and freshly ground black pepper to taste
1	lemon, quartered for garnish

Combine the lamb with the cayenne, cumin, cinnamon, and with half of the onions and parsley. Work with your hands until just mixed, being careful not to overwork the meat. Roll into small meatballs, a bit smaller than golf balls, but bigger than a gumball.

Bring a large pot of salted water to a boil. Add the Israeli couscous and cook until just shy of al dente. Drain and drizzle with enough oil to lightly coat the pearls and keep them from sticking together.

Set a large sauté pan over medium-high heat and add the butter. Add the remaining onion, the ginger, chile, and saffron, and sauté until the onion begins to caramelize. Stir in the cilantro, lemon juice, and water. Season with salt and pepper. Increase the heat and bring to a boil. Drop in the meatballs, cover, and reduce the heat. Poach gently, stirring occasionally, for about 20 minutes, or until cooked through. Add the cooked couscous to the pan, stirring gently to distribute. Cook, uncovered, until the couscous is perfectly cooked through and the sauce has thickened slightly. Sprinkle with the remaining parsley, and serve with crusty bread and a wedge of lemon.

"He kissed me under the Moorish wall and I thought well as well him as another and then I asked him with my eyes to ask again *yes* and then he asked me would I *yes* to say *yes* my mountain flower and first I put my arms around him *yes* and drew him down to me as he could feel my breasts all perfume *yes* and his heart was going like mad and *yes* I said *yes* I will *Yes*."

James Joyce, *Ulysses* (1922)

petals in white chocolate

vibrant colors captured in ivory

"To be honest, I had been seeing Jessica for a while and was ready for a little more, if you know what I mean. A friend of mine suggested I make her dinner, followed by a dessert bouquet of petals in white chocolate. During the course of the evening, I managed to spill wine on my carefully-chosen shirt, kitchen heat flattened my much worked-on hair, and the chicken tasted rubbery. Thankfully, Jessica was so moved by my efforts and the sweet little candies I made that she forgave the mishaps of earlier and gave me some sweet little candies of her own." *John, on impressing Jessica, third week of dating, Boston, MA*

YIELDS 10 CANDIES

Edible blossoms, such as unsprayed begonias, geraniums, lilacs, daisies, Johnny jump-ups, pansies, honeysuckle, roses, tulips, borage, lavender, violets, and pinks

10 bonbon cups

3 ounces high-quality white chocolate, finely chopped

If using larger flowers, pluck the petals and place 1 to 4 petals, pretty-side down, in each bonbon cup. If using tiny flowers like Johnny jump-ups or small violets, place the whole blossom, face down, into the cups. The blossoms need to lie as flat as possible.

Melt the chocolate in a double boiler over hot, not boiling, water. Alternatively, microwave on 50 percent power, 1 minute at a time, stirring frequently until smooth.

Carefully fill each cup halfway with the melted chocolate. Chill for up to 4 hours to let the chocolate set. Peel off the cups and arrange on a serving plate (or the body) to showcase the petals.

hibiscus cooler

utterly refreshing

Says Richard on this summer spritzer, "I was suddenly seized with a desire to shuffle." His wife, Marie, was suddenly seized with a desire to smile.

YIELDS 4 SERVINGS

1 quart water, divided

½ cup dried hibiscus blossoms, sometimes labeled "jamaica" in Latino markets

1 cup sugar

1 tablespoon sliced fresh ginger

4 limes, divided

Place 2 cups of water, the hibiscus blossoms, sugar, ginger, and the zest of 1 lime in a medium saucepan set over medium-high heat and stir. Bring to a boil, and then turn off the heat and let steep for 15 minutes, or until the hibiscus has infused the water with flavor and color.

Pour the remaining water in a pitcher and add the juice of 3 limes, including the zested lime. Strain the hibiscus mixture into the pitcher. Thinly slice the remaining lime into small rounds and float in the pitcher for garnish. Chill at least 2 hours and serve over ice.

stuffed squash blossoms

one of summer's special treats

Olive oil for greasing

20 freshly picked squash blossoms, pesticide free

1 small shallot, finely minced

2 cloves garlic, finely minced

1 small bunch fresh cilantro, finely minced

⅓ cup finely chopped toasted pine nuts

¼ cup panko or breadcrumbs

1 (3-ounce) log goat cheese, softened

1 large ball fresh mozzarella, shredded or finely diced

Salt and freshly ground black pepper

1 small red Serrano chile, finely chopped

2 tablespoons unsalted butter, melted

"It was a hot summer day when we made these stuffed squash blossoms using extra flowers from a neighbor's over-producing plant. We fed each other hot bundles straight from the oven. The blossoms had been made translucent with the butter and the heat, and though they seemed so delicate, breaking through the resilient skins with our teeth was harder than it seemed."
Gwyneth and Tomás, Albuquerque, NM

For this dish, you'll need to make friends with a gardener. If he grows squash, he'll have blossoms on hand for much of the summer. Otherwise, head to your local farmer's market, as you'll rarely find them in traditional grocery stores. Still, these flowers are the sex organs of the plant, bursting with color and form and texture. They're worth your effort.

If preparing this for two, pick whatever quantity of squash blossoms you think you'll need (6, 8, maybe even 10). Put your partner on blossom duty: Gently prying apart the flower's tangled folds will have him searching for ants, but thinking of the birds and the bees. You can stuff the blossoms ahead of time, and then bake just before serving with some chilled gazpacho. Save the remaining cheese for a fabulous apéro – top your favorite crackers, pipe into celery stalks, dip with crispy breadsticks. Or, spread in a small casserole or crock and bake until hot and bubbly for a dip.

YIELDS 4 TO 6 SERVINGS

Preheat the oven to 425 degrees. Grease a 13 x 9 x 2-inch baking dish with the olive oil.

Remove the pistil from the flowers with scissors. Check for ants or other insects if the blossoms come from your garden. Brush them away, but do not wash. Thoroughly combine the shallot, garlic, cilantro, pine nuts, panko, goat cheese, mozzarella, salt, pepper, and chile in a small bowl.

Spread the cheese mixture on a cutting board to form a square that's about ¾-inch thick. Using a sharp knife, cut the square into 20 pieces by slicing 4 columns and 5 rows.

Scrape 1 square of the stuffing onto a butter knife. Delicately open each squash blossom and stuff with the cheese mixture. Twist the petals to close the flower and place in the baking dish. Repeat the process with the rest of the blossoms. Brush the flowers with melted butter and bake for 10 to 15 minutes, or until the cheese is melted and warmed through. Serve immediately.

orange blossom panna cotta

a silky-soft pillow of cream

"She described it as creamy, silky and decadent . . . and apparently the panna cotta turned out okay too. We even had it again for dessert the following night, this time with fresh blackberries, which were equally delicious. With the blackberries, we were able to pick them up and feed them to each other, which was a bit harder to manage with the slippery peaches. Either way, it's definitely a dish you want to close your eyes and savor." *Matt and Josie, together 10 years, Kansas City, MO*

"After three years of dating and a year of living together, I'm lucky to get more than a 'wow' for anything I make – and I can cook! But the silky, jiggly panna cotta with its crown of glistening peaches and vibrant rose petals elicited open-mouthed awe." *Kelli and Jim, dating 3 years, co-habitating for 1, New York, NY*

Orange blossom water is available in some grocery stores and in most Middle Eastern and Indian grocers. As an alternative, you can steep a few strips of orange zest in a bit of hot water until infused, about 20 minutes. It won't be the same, but it will lend a mild, sweet orange flavor to the peaches and panna cotta. For a little variety, try replacing the orange blossom water with rose water, and the edible flowers with pesticide-free rose petals. Sprinkle a few extra petals heading toward the bedroom or garden tub for extra flourish.

- 2 tablespoons cold water
- 1/2 tablespoon unflavored gelatin (about 1/2 envelope)
- 1 cup heavy cream
- 1/2 cup half-and-half
- 2 tablespoons plus 2 teaspoons sugar
- 2 1/2 tablespoons orange blossom water, divided
- 4 ripe peaches, peeled and diced
- 4 to 8 edible violets or other purple flowers, pesticide free

YIELDS 4 TO 6 SERVINGS

Place the water in a small bowl and sprinkle with the gelatin. Let sit 10 minutes to soften.

Set a large saucepan over medium-high heat, and add the cream, half-and-half, and sugar. Bring to a boil, stirring frequently, until the sugar is dissolved. Remove the pan from the heat and add the gelatin mixture and 1 1/2 tablespoons of the orange blossom water, stirring to dissolve the gelatin completely. Pour the cream mixture into 4 ramekins or pretty serving glasses, and cool to room temperature. Cover and chill at least 6 hours or overnight for the panna cotta to set.

Just before serving, place the diced peaches in a small bowl and drizzle with the remaining tablespoon of orange blossom water. Stir gently to distribute the flavor.

To serve, fill a mixing bowl with hot water. Dip each ramekin in the hot water for several seconds and run a knife around the edge to loosen the cream from the sides. Place a serving dish on top of the ramekin and invert. Or, serve the panna cotta directly in the ramekin and avoid the cumbersome unmolding process altogether. Place a small mound of peaches on top of the panna cotta and sprinkle more peaches around the plate. Garnish with an edible blossom.

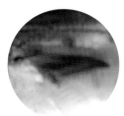

s e a f o o d

Ever since Aphrodite rose from the sea on a scalloped shell amid the foaming waves of the ocean, seafood has been a credible aphrodisiac. • Men in the West Indies value conch for its "strengthening" powers. • France's King Henry IV had his chef keep a pot of eel simmering on the stove at all times, just in case he was in the mood, but couldn't muster enough energy to see his adventure through. • George H. Napheys, M.D., wrote about fish's aphrodisiac powers in 1871, asserting that coastal men were unusually salacious, most likely due to seafood's peculiar tonic influence over those with diets high in seafood. • Now we know that the "peculiar tonic influence" comes from seafood's rich nutrient base of protein, iron, zinc, and iodine. Protein makes for healthier muscles, while iron helps with the production of healthy red blood cells, increasing stamina in the process. Zinc increases testosterone, and semen is positively loaded with the mineral. Iodine, the powerhouse of the body, feeds the thyroid gland. Translated into aphrodisiac-speak: Lack of iodine makes you feel sluggish. Ample iodine makes you feel vivacious, energetic, passionate.

harissa-spiced tilapia cakes with cucumber salad

moroccan-influenced flavors

for the cucumber salad:

Juice of 1 orange

Juice of ½ lemon

1 tablespoon orange blossom water, or more to taste

½ teaspoon ground cinnamon (optional)

2 cucumbers, peeled, seeded, and chopped

Salt to taste

for the harissa mayonnaise:

½ cup mayonnaise

1 tablespoon harissa or nuoc cham*

for the tilapia cakes:

Hefty pinch of saffron

1 pound tilapia

2 teaspoons harissa or nuoc cham*

Zest of ½ preserved lemon, minced (or regular lemon if preserved is unavailable)

½ bunch fresh cilantro, minced

1 tablespoon minced garlic

1 large egg

Salt and freshly ground black pepper to taste

Grapeseed oil for frying

"We felt like we were on a roller coaster of the senses while preparing this meal. Bright citrus flavors, fragrant orange flower water, warming cinnamon, spicy harissa, and the yellow-orange colors seeping from the saffron threads. Frying up the fish cakes was the best part, because it's quick and dirty, and suddenly it's dinnertime." *Anneliese and Danny, Atlanta, GA*

"Cooking with a romantic partner is often a sexy experience in its own right. Like a dance where taste buds are teased until flavors come together at the climax that is the meal itself. But cooking the tilapia cakes and preparing the cucumber salad literally became a dance. Because of its dualistic nature, this recipe was a tag-team effort that had us shimmying toward each other and away as we spiced things up in the kitchen. The resultant meal (paired with liberal amounts of both Frank Sinatra and Spanish red wine) was a highly sensual fusion of heat kissed by coolness, of spice tempered by innocence. Edwin said I was the sexiest chef he'd ever seen, and when the meal was over, he kissed me and kissed me with lips seasoned with nuoc cham." *Christa and Edwin, together 4 years and practically engaged, Boston, MA*

The cinnamon completely changes the flavor profile of this salad. Anneliese and Danny described it exactly as I tasted it, and I love the play of flavors it creates on the tongue. But if you're not a fan of cinnamon, leave it out, as it easily takes center stage over the other spices and ingredients. Don't stress, either, if you can't find the orange blossom water. It adds a wonderful floral note, but the salad works just as well without it. You'll have best luck finding it in Middle Eastern or Indian markets.

YIELDS 3 OR 4 SERVINGS

To prepare the cucumber salad, combine the orange juice, lemon juice, and orange flower water in a small bowl. If you like cinnamon, add it as well. Add the cucumber and a pinch of salt, and stir to combine. Taste and add more salt if needed. Cover and refrigerate until ready to use.

For the mayonnaise, combine the mayonnaise and harissa in a small bowl and refrigerate until ready to use.

For the tilapia cakes, soak the saffron in a teaspoon of water to soften. Cut the fish into manageable chunks and place in a food processor. Add the saffron and its water, (continued) the harissa, preserved lemon zest, cilantro, garlic, and egg. Pulse several times until the ingredients are just combined, but still slightly chunky.

Line a baking sheet with waxed paper and fill a small bowl with water. Wet your hands and shape the mixture into patties about 2½ inches in diameter by ¾-inch tall. (You'll have 8 to 10 cakes.) For more uniform patties, dip a standard ¼-cup measuring cup in the water to wet it and keep the mixture from sticking. Fill the measuring cup with the tilapia mixture and smooth over with a spatula. Invert the tilapia cake onto the waxed paper, tapping the cup if it doesn't come out easily. Continue with the remaining tilapia, always wetting your measuring cup in between. (The cakes can be made up to 2 hours ahead. Cover tightly and refrigerate until ready to fry.)

Preheat the oven to 200 degrees to keep the finished cakes warm. Set a large, heavy skillet over medium to medium-high heat and fill with enough oil to nicely coat the entire bottom. When the oil is hot but not smoking, gently place the tilapia cakes in the pan, being careful not to overcrowd. Pan fry until golden brown on both sides and cooked through, about 2 to 3 minutes per side. Drain on paper towels and add more oil between batches if necessary. Keep warm in the oven on a wire rack set over a baking sheet until ready to serve.

To serve, place the tilapia cakes on plates. Top each cake with a dollop of harissa mayonnaise and spoon with some of the cucumber salad and its juices. Serve immediately, while the cakes are still hot and the salad is still cold.

* If harissa is unavailable, use the ubiquitous Vietnamese chile sauce nuoc cham found on restaurant tables across the country. It comes in a plastic squeeze bottle with a green lid and a rooster on the front. Both are chile sauces. The harissa will give more of a Tunisian slant to the dish, while the nuoc cham will taste more Asian.

honey-glazed salmon

a simple treatment for a beautiful fish

Olive oil for greasing

2　(6-ounce) salmon fillets, about 1½ inches thick

Salt and freshly ground black pepper to taste

2　teaspoons honey

2　teaspoons chopped basil

Aaron likes, rather loves, salmon. Remember his experience at the cafe in the Village? (See page 47 for reference.) Well, in follow-up, they decided to rendezvous in New York again. He flew in from Texas, she from Boston. They were to meet at a hip New York restaurant, not having seen each other since that night at the cafe six months before. In Aaron's words, "She ran into the restaurant, 30 minutes late, soaking wet from the rain, with luggage in tow. Once she regrouped and warmed up, I ordered the baked salmon and she ordered a noodle-basket with shrimp called Aphrodisiac Love Nest. Hubba hubba. I'm not telling any more, but yes, I do still call her." [*Update: Aaron has not heard from Dominique since 1998. When he looked her up a few years ago before a business trip to Boston, he was unable to find her. Life has moved on, apparently for the both of them. He still enjoys the story that is her.*]

YIELDS 2 SERVINGS

Preheat the oven to 350 degrees. Pour a bit of oil in a baking dish large enough to accommodate the salmon, and tilt to distribute the oil around the bottom of the dish. Place the salmon, skin-side down, in the baking dish. Pat the flesh dry, and season with salt and pepper. Drizzle with the honey and smear with your fingers to coat evenly. Top with the basil. Bake for 15 minutes, or until the desired degree of doneness.

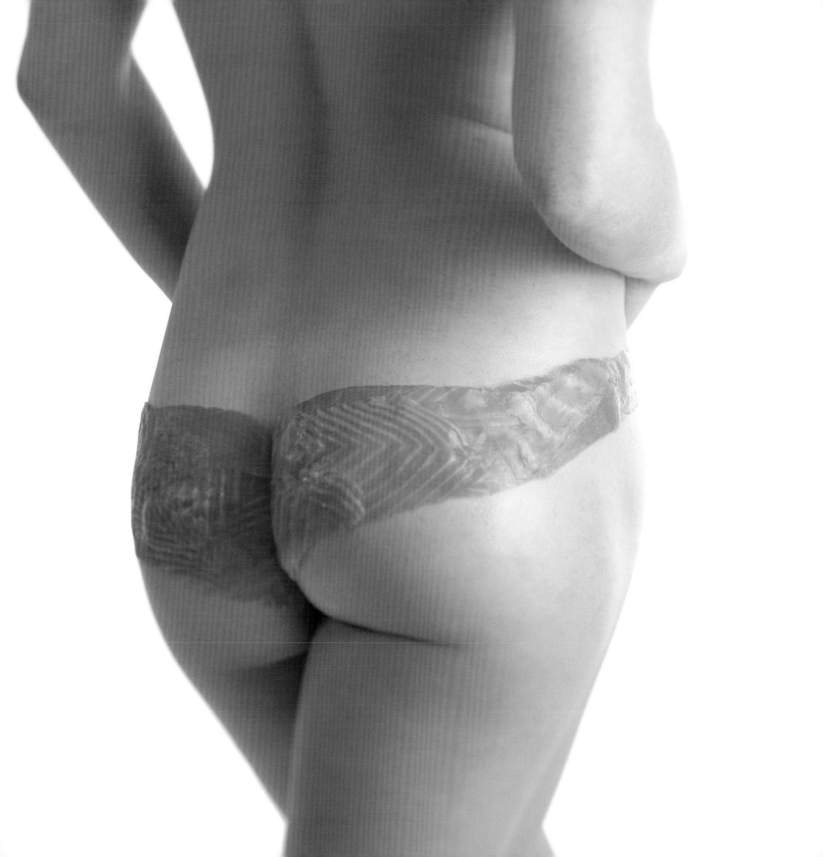

halibut brandade

fluffy potatoes with flaky white fish

for the halibut:

1   pound fresh halibut or cod

1   medium onion, chopped

6   whole black peppercorns

2   whole cloves

2   bay leaves

1½ teaspoons salt

for the brandade:

1   large baking potato, peeled
    and quartered lengthwise

3   cloves garlic, minced to a
    paste with a bit of salt, plus
    1 clove for seasoning bread

1   tablespoon minced
    fresh rosemary

¾   cup extra-virgin olive oil

    Salt and freshly ground
    black pepper

    Freshly squeezed lemon
    juice to taste

    Baguette rounds for dipping

"The brandade was simply wonderful – we loved the texture of the crispy top with the creamy interior. The next day, we formed the leftovers into small balls (about the size of golf balls) and fried them in olive oil. We rolled some in panko and left the others plain. How simple, but how good! Even Rubicon and Memphis, our Rhodesian Ridgebacks, got in on the act, stealing a large portion of the baguette I had smeared with the brandade. We didn't see them again until morning."
Robert and Heather, Salinas, CA

YIELDS 4 SERVINGS

To poach the halibut, place a large saucepan over high heat and pour in 1 cup of water. Add the onion, peppercorns, cloves, bay leaves, and salt, and bring to a boil. Reduce the heat, cover, and simmer for 10 minutes to infuse the water with the seasonings.

Add 4 cups cold water and the halibut to the pan. Adjust the heat to medium or medium-high. Watch carefully: When the water barely starts simmering, immediately remove the pan from the heat. Cover and let poach for 10 minutes. Remove the fish from the pot with a slotted spoon, and use the liquid to cook the potato.

To make the brandade, bring the poaching liquid back to a boil and add the potato. Cook 10 minutes, or until completely soft.

Preheat the broiler. Cut the halibut into 1-inch pieces, removing any stray bones or dark skin. Place the halibut, garlic, potato, and rosemary in a food processor and pulse until just mixed. With the motor running, add the olive oil. The consistency should be similar to fluffy mashed potatoes or a thick mousse. Season with salt, pepper, and lemon juice to taste.

Spread the brandade in a 13 x 9 x 2-inch gratin dish or a 9 x 9 x 2-inch casserole. Make a grid on top of the brandade with the tines of a fork for an attractive finish. Place under the broiler and bake for 3 to 5 minutes, or until golden brown on top. Serve immediately with slices of country bread or baguette that have been toasted and rubbed with a garlic clove.

crab quesadillas with ripe peach salsa

cream cheese anchors the sweet crabmeat

"We put the simple dish together: You slather that; I'll squirt this. The silky textures melded together, cream cheese into crab into avocado. The slight bite of tomatillo and lime. The tanginess of homemade peach and pepper salsa. Ripe flavors for hot summer days. After dinner, foot rubs all around."
Lesley and Ted, 10 years and counting, Pasadena, CA

"We were suffering through yet another stifling July evening when we decided to try this recipe. Quick, simple, wouldn't overheat the kitchen – it seemed perfect. Sitting at my tiny table, we hungrily ate the first batch, giggling at the crab-lime juice dripping down our faces and hands. For the second batch, we got a tad overexcited applying the hot sauce and were rapidly overcome by the heat in and around us. I flopped on the bed, still licking my fingers, and lazily watched Tim install the air conditioner that had been sitting unused in my closet for the past eight months. We lay on the bed together, letting the cold air blow over us, until it was time to heat up all over again." *Tim and Jessie, dating 2 years, Denver, CO*

If cooking for just you and your honey, assemble only three quesadillas and save the rest for a light "morning-after" lunch. Combine the remaining cream filling ingredients, and save one whole avocado. The next day, slice the avocado in half, remove the pit and peel, and stuff with the crab salad.

YIELDS 6 QUESADILLAS

To make the salsa, combine all the ingredients in a small bowl. Refrigerate until ready to use.

Slice each avocado in half lengthwise. Remove the pit. Set the avocado on the counter and make thin slices lengthwise through the flesh. Scoop out the sliced halves with a spoon. Combine the cream cheese and cilantro until the cilantro is distributed evenly. Spread a layer of cream cheese over one entire side of each tortilla. Place a few pieces of tomatillos over half the tortilla, then top with some crab meat. Squirt some fresh lime juice over the crab meat, season with salt and pepper, and top with a single layer of avocado slices. Fold over the tortilla, pressing down lightly so everything stays in place. It will look like a half moon.

Set a large nonstick skillet over medium heat. Add a scant teaspoon of olive oil and swirl around the pan. Add 2 quesadillas to the pan and cover. Cook 2 to 3 minutes, and then peek to see if the underside is starting to brown. If nicely toasted on one side, flip and continue to cook on the other side until golden brown. Slice in half for easy eating and serve with the peach salsa.

for the peach salsa:

- 2 peaches or 1 large mango, peeled and chopped
- ½ small jalapeño, seeded and minced
- ½ small red onion, minced
- ½ small red bell pepper, seeded and minced
- 1 to 2 tablespoons chopped fresh cilantro
- 2 slices tomatillo, minced
- 1 to 2 cloves garlic, minced
  Juice and zest of 1 lime
  Salt and freshly ground pepper to taste

for the quesadillas:

- 2 medium avocados
- 4 ounces cream cheese, softened
- 2 tablespoons chopped fresh cilantro
- 6 (6-inch) flour tortillas, preferably freshly made from the grocery or a restaurant
- 1 tomatillo, husked, washed, thinly sliced, and peel removed
- 1 (8-ounce) container high-quality crabmeat (no imitation allowed!), picked over for shells
- 2 limes
  Salt and freshly ground black pepper to taste
- 4 teaspoons olive oil, if needed

fish tacos with avocado crema and jícama slaw

armchair travel to the baja coast

for the slaw:

1 tablespoon Dijon mustard

   Juice of 2 limes (¼ cup)

   Salt and freshly ground
   black pepper to taste

¼ cup extra-virgin olive oil

¾ cup shredded jícama

¾ cup shredded purple or
   Napa cabbage

¼ cup shredded carrots
   (1 or 2 carrots)

2 tablespoons shredded
   red onion

for the crema:

1 avocado

½ cup Mexican crema or
   sour cream

½ teaspoon salt

   Zest and juice of half a lime

   Green Tabasco to taste

2 tablespoons chopped cilantro

"Keep in mind, fish tacos and I go way back to Las Olas in San Diego, eaten on a sandy beach at sunset . . . the anticipation of cooking together made us both giddy just getting to the kitchen. Cooking, playing, tasting the dressing and crema off each other's fingers . . . it could've gotten out of hand, but the recipe requires just enough attention, especially with the hot oil, that it makes it a little difficult to actually play grab-ass in the kitchen. That's okay – there was plenty of time for that later. Over tacos, we discussed our dream location for consuming these and then each other. The unanimous decision? A deck overlooking the ocean with a cool breeze blowing through." *Victoria and Keifel, married 5 years, Nashville, TN*

"My husband and I find the kitchen to be the center of the home, the place most likely for romance to ignite. As we prep a new dinner recipe together, we simmer in the sauce of anticipation of pairing the mysterious blend of flavors. Each reference to pinch or grind stirs our desires. Wine, candles, and our daily "teasing" make dinner prep the perfect place for a romantic interlude. Of note: This fish keeps well in a warm oven if things heat up and dinner must be postponed." *Debbie and Dave do dinner!, partners for 9 years, newlyweds for 1 year, Grapevine, TX*

YIELDS 3 TO 4 SERVINGS

To prepare the slaw, combine the mustard and lime juice in a large mixing bowl. Season with salt and pepper to taste. Drizzle in the olive oil, whisking constantly until emulsified. Add the jícama, cabbage, carrots, and onion. (You can quickly grate all these ingredients using a food processor, but I prefer the chunkier, more free-form effect of hand-cutting. For even faster results, use the 8-ounce bagged coleslaw available in most produce sections.) Toss to coat thoroughly with the vinaigrette, and refrigerate until ready to use. (continued)

To prepare the crema, combine all the ingredients in a tall bowl or glass and purée with an immersion blender. The crema can be made up to 6 hours in advance; refrigerate until ready to use. Alternatively, if time is an issue, skip the crema and use fresh avocado slices instead.

To prepare the fish, set a large saucepan over medium-high heat and fill with enough oil to come halfway up the sides. Heat to 350 degrees, or until a drop of batter sizzles and floats to the top. Preheat the oven to 200 degrees and add the stack of corn tortillas to warm.

Cut the fish into bite-size pieces and season with salt and pepper. Whisk together the beer, egg, flour, and Tabasco in a medium mixing bowl to create a batter. Add the fish to the batter, coating well. Place the fish in the hot oil, one piece at a time, and fry for 3 to 5 minutes, or until golden brown on all sides. Drain on paper towels. Keep warm in the oven on a wire rack set above a baking sheet until ready to assemble the tacos.

To assemble the tacos, place 2 to 3 morsels of fish on each corn tortilla. Top with the crunchy slaw and drizzle with the avocado crema. Serve immediately.

for the tacos:

Peanut or grapeseed oil for frying

10 corn tortillas

1 pound fresh cod or catfish

Salt and freshly ground black pepper to taste

1 cup Corona beer, or other beer of choice

1 large egg

1 cup all-purpose flour

3 drops Tabasco, or more to taste

p i n e   n u t s

Reatimus used them on the Romans. Galen, a second-century Greek doctor, prescribed them to his patients for their reported powers. Even today, some people hail the pine nut as one very deft kernel of love. • Pine nuts, also called pignolis, come from inside the cones of pine trees. This delicate and buttery nut, obtained with quite a struggle by drying the cone, comes in several varieties: Europeans eat an Italian or Swiss version; Asians use the strongly-flavored Chinese nut; Americans eat a Mexican nut. • But it is the communities around the north-western Himalayas who rejoice the most. Privy to the pignoli of pignolis, a product of the Chilgoza Pine, they enjoy an outstanding birthrate. Perhaps pine nuts increase fertility. Or maybe they just increase copulation. Whatever the case, they're worth a try.

buttermilk-pine nut pie

a twist on grandmother's chess pie

2 cups sugar

1 stick unsalted butter, softened

3 large eggs

3 tablespoons unsalted flour

½ teaspoon salt

1 cup buttermilk

½ teaspoon lemon extract

1 (9-inch) circle refrigerated pie dough, preferably Pillsbury's Just Unroll!

1 cup pine nuts, toasted

"It was my third date with Josie. There had been sparks between us, but the circumstances hadn't allowed us to act on them the first two times. (At least, that was my read on the whole thing.) This time, I was cooking her dinner at my apartment, so I knew if anything was going to happen between us, this was it. She came over a little early, so I gave her a glass of wine and told her to make herself at home. She asked if she could play a CD. I told her sure, whatever she wanted to hear. She picked the Cowboy Junkies. In my mind, I was going 'Yes!' Then she came in the kitchen and sat on the counter. I'd just pulled the pie out the oven. She commented on how good it smelled, so I offered her a bite. I cut a little wedge and put it on a fork and started to hand it to her, warning her that it was hot. She then grabbed my hand with the fork in it and proceeded to blow on the food, her eyes never leaving me the whole time. I thought I was going to die. I cut off another piece. This time, she grabbed the fork out of my hand, blew on the food, took it in her fingers, and placed it in my mouth. Her fingers were on my lips, and I started to lick them off. This was followed by a kiss laced in honey. Needless to say, things heated up and dinner had to be reheated. And I'm glad to report we've been 'cooking' ever since." *Billy's words on pine nut pie and that crucial third date with Josie, together 4 months, Kansas City, MO*

YIELDS 6 TO 8 SERVINGS

Preheat the oven to 350 degrees. Combine the sugar and butter in a large mixing bowl with an electric mixer until light and fluffy. Add the eggs, one at a time, combining between each addition. Combine the flour and salt on a paper towel, and add to the mixture. Stir in the buttermilk and lemon extract. Unroll the pie dough and line an 8-inch pie pan with the crust. Spread the pine nuts over the bottom of the crust. Pour the buttermilk mixture over the pine nuts. Bake in the oven for 2 hours, or until the top is golden brown and the center is just barely set. Cover lightly with foil if the edges start to darken too quickly.

homemade pie crusts: Homemade crusts taste notably superior to store-bought ones. If you want to make your own, cut 2 sticks of cold butter into small pieces and place in a small bowl. Cut ¼ cup of shortening into small pieces. Add to the butter and place in the refrigerator. (Good crusts require cold ingredients.) (continued)

Place 1¼ cups cake flour, 1¼ cups all-purpose flour, and 1 teaspoon salt in a food processor. Pulse to combine. Add the chilled butter and shortening. Pulse just until the fats are cut into the flour and resemble little peas. Add a little bit of ice water and pulse again. Take off the lid and touch the dough. Do the flour and butter come together between your fingers? If not, add a little more water and pulse again. Be careful not overprocess, or you'll have a tough crust. Pour the dough out onto a clean work surface and knead 2 to 3 times, just to bring all the flour into the dough. Divide in half and form into two flat disks. Wrap with plastic wrap, and refrigerate until ready to roll out.

blueberry-pine nut crumble

wild blueberries taste even more intense

"Anything to make those dimples appear, and the blueberries seemed to do it, so I piled them on, hot and juicy from the oven, melting the ice cream as fast as his eyes were melting my . . . Well, anyway, we had to sit very close to share dessert from the same bowl — all sweet, tart, hot, and cold at once, and so I must say thank you berries for leading to that first sweet kiss." *Heather and Kris, first date, Austin, TX*

YIELDS 2 LARGE SERVINGS

Preheat the oven to 350 degrees. Rinse and pick over the berries; drain in a colander. Toss in the zest and ginger and mix gently with your hands to coat.

Crush the pine nuts with the flat of a large knife or with the base of a sturdy drinking glass. In a small bowl, combine the granola, nuts, butter, and maple syrup. Gently fold the mixture together with a spatula, creating large crumbles of topping.

Divide the berries between two 6-ounce ramekins and divide the topping between the two, pressing it down on top of the berries. Set the ramekins on a baking sheet and bake until the fruit is bubbly and hot, about 25 minutes, taking care not to let the crumble topping burn. Serve hot with crème fraîche or vanilla ice cream.

1   pint fresh blueberries

Zest of one lemon,
or more to taste

½-inch piece fresh ginger,
peeled and grated

2   tablespoons pine nuts

1   cup crunchy granola,
any variety

2   tablespoons unsalted butter,
sliced and slightly softened

1½ tablespoons maple syrup

Crème fraîche or vanilla ice
cream for topping

It's true!

Take Don and Falina . . . Typical casual long-term dating situation — no commitment, no time frames, nothing. Bowling league. Movies. Party attendance. Enter pine nuts, served innocently one evening in some unassuming pesto. Bam! All the sudden they're married,

Falina's mother swears on her rosary and complains that Don and Falina could have taken a larger jumbo mortgage if they had listened to her in the first place. Pine nuts, apparently, run in the family.

More evidence? Fine. Look at Heidi and Paul. Classic in vitro cataclysm.

anecdotal research says pine nuts

have two and a half children, and arrange a jumbo mortgage they never plan to pay. And they're not even American! Pine nuts, of course.

Now, you're thinking, "That's pretty sketchy to conclude cause-and-effect. How can you be sure it was pine nuts?" Trust me on this. The doctor says so, reluctantly. The psychoanalyst confers.

Over and over and over until Paul said one more magazine and specimen container and he was giving up, period. Heidi was in tears, walking around so very carefully after visiting the doctor, who by the way, has never failed so utterly. So they start reading fringe literature to get out of the house because . . . well, you know. Molasses.

Wheat germ. Moon phases. Vigorous exercise. Complete bed rest. The Dali Lama. The Hotel Nikko in Chicago, from which they steal a copy of *The Teaching of Buddha* that prepares them for their visit with the Dali Lama. Anti-gravity positions. Anti-gravity positions in simulated weightlessness environments.

just don't appreciate neighbors, you know.) The result: Twins, non-identical.

Dave and Georgette. Helen and François. Jeremy and Jo Ann. Vern and Kelly. Debbie and Tracy. Miles and Michelle. Jennifer and John. Marie and Bobby.

But hey. I'm not going to beat my

enhance nesting instinct and fertility.

Career changes. Scheduled intercourse. Varicose vein readings for fertility. Name it. Imagine it.

You guessed it. Pine nuts. And it only took one can over the course of a week, servings at breakfast and before, well, bed. Falina's mother shook her head in disbelief that Heidi's mother didn't call her sooner to confide. (People these days

head against the wall over this pine nut thing. Just try them. Toss them into salad or pasta whole, chop them up into dust and put them in your protein drink at the gym, roast them, toast them, juice them, crush them against your soft palate until your tongue hurts.

I guarantee pine nuts will work for you, too. So does Falina's mother.

Pine nuts according to Barry McCann, Colorado Springs, CO

mediterranean rice salad

fresh taste for a picnic lunch

2½ tablespoons olive oil, divided

½ cup basmati rice

¾ cup chicken broth

¼ cup Kalamata olives, minced

Juice and zest of ½ small lemon

1 handful fresh arugula or watercress, chopped

1 green onion, minced

¼ cup pine nuts, toasted

¼ cup feta cheese, finely crumbled

Freshly ground black pepper to taste

"When all else fails, I buy Drew some Kalamata olives. He can eat them by the gallon-full it seems. I, on the other hand, can tolerate them. We found this Mediterranean rice salad a happy compromise – he got his olives and I got . . . well, let's just say the evening wasn't exactly the pits."

Carrie and Drew, dating 2 years, Portland, OR

YIELDS 2 TO 3 SERVINGS

Heat 1½ tablespoons of the olive oil in a medium sauce pan set over medium-high heat. Sauté the rice, stirring frequently, until fragrant and toasty. Pour in the broth and bring to a boil.

Stir, cover the pan, and reduce the heat to low. Cook 15 minutes, or until all the liquid is absorbed and the rice is tender. Fluff with a fork and spoon into a large bowl. Stir in the remaining tablespoon of olive oil. Add the olives, lemon juice, arugula, green onion, pine nuts, cheese, and pepper to taste. Serve warm or at room temperature with grilled pork or chilled rare roast beef.

veal medallions
with pine nuts and herbs

serve with fresh bread to soak up any extra sauce

"I'd been seeing Derek for quite some time, and the relationship had reached a comfortable, if unexciting, stage. I decided to go for an all-out aphrodisiac meal, with the highlight being the supremely elegant entrée of veal medallions with pine nuts and herbs. I didn't tell him it was an aphrodisiac meal – I was just curious to see if they actually worked or if it were more psychological than anything. We ate until we were stuffed, moved over to the couch with our wine, and in usual fashion, turned on the tube and fell asleep. Alas, the meal had not worked. Or so I thought. Around 1:00 a.m., T.V. still blaring and dishes still dirty, I was awakened by soft, fluttery kisses. The kind I used to get every morning, but hadn't felt in probably three months. I guess there is something to it after all, but Derek's getting a bit suspicious about my increased interest in cooking."

Janet reflects on the power of veal medallions over Derek, together 6 years, Raleigh, NC

YIELDS 2 SERVINGS

2	(12-ounce) veal rib chops, boned and trimmed
	Salt and freshly ground black pepper to taste
2	tablespoons olive oil, divided
2	tomatoes, peeled, seeded, and chopped
¼	cup pine nuts, toasted
1	tablespoon capers
1	shallot, minced
1	clove garlic, crushed
½	tablespoon chopped fresh basil, plus several whole leaves for garnish
½	teaspoon dried oregano
2	tablespoons dry white wine
½	tablespoon freshly squeezed lemon juice
1	tablespoon butter, chilled

Preheat the oven to 200 degrees to keep the finished chops warm. Generously season the veal chops with salt and pepper. Set a large skillet over medium-high heat and add 1 tablespoon of olive oil. When hot, add the veal chops to the pan and do not disturb. After 3 or 4 minutes, peek to see if the chops have browned. When nicely browned, flip over and let cook until browned on the other side. Place the chops on an oven-safe plate and set in the oven to keep warm.

Pour the remaining tablespoon of olive oil into the skillet and add the tomatoes, pine nuts, capers, shallot, garlic, basil, and oregano. Cook for 10 minutes, or until the shallot is translucent. Increase the heat to high and add the wine and lemon juice, gently scraping the bottom of the pan to release any flavorful browned bits. Simmer about 4 minutes, or until the sauce has reduced slightly. Remove the veal from the oven and pour any released juices into the sauce.

To serve, place one veal chop on each plate. Swirl the cold butter into the sauce for a silky finish. Pour the pan sauce evenly over the chops, and garnish with several leaves of basil.

angel hair pasta with fresh fennel pesto

a wonderful dish from jeff lehr's collection

While the pesto rests and the flavors mingle, take some time to do the same with your lover. Be sure to save some energy for "dessert" – this sensuous feast may bring a glow you haven't felt before . . .

YIELDS 3 SERVINGS

for the pasta:

¾ cup boiling water

1½ cups sun-dried tomatoes

½ small bulb of fennel, thinly sliced, divided

1 clove garlic

¼ cup pine nuts

¼ cup fresh basil leaves

1 tablespoon fresh oregano leaves or ½ teaspoon dried

½ tablespoon freshly squeezed lemon juice

½ teaspoon sea salt, or more to taste

1½ tablespoons olive oil

8 ounces angel hair pasta

for garnish:

Roasted pine nuts

Sliced ripe olives

Freshly grated Parmesan cheese

Freshly ground black pepper

Fresh oregano leaves

Fresh basil leaves

Pour boiling water over the tomatoes; allow to sit until soft and pliable, about 5 to 8 minutes. Drain, reserving liquid.

Combine one-fourth of the fennel with the tomatoes, garlic, pine nuts, basil, oregano, lemon juice, salt, and olive oil in a food processor or blender. Process until smooth, adding the reserved tomato-soaking water a bit at a time until the desired consistency is reached. Allow to rest while preparing pasta; if possible, let the flavors blend 30 to 60 minutes.

Bring a large pot of salted water to boil over high heat. Cook the pasta according to package directions until al dente; drain. Combine with the fennel pesto in a large mixing bowl, tossing to mix evenly. To serve, mound pasta in the center of 2 or 3 plates, scatter with the remaining fennel, and garnish to your heart's content.

arabian couscous with pine nuts and raisins

works beautifully next to roasted meats

According to Kevin, "This dish benefits significantly when prepared by a cook dressed only in an apron, tied loosely around the waist."

YIELDS 2 TO 3 SERVINGS

Melt the butter in a saucepan set over medium heat. Add the onion and carrot; sauté until onions are translucent, about 5 minutes. Add the stock and raisins. Raise the heat to high and bring the liquid to a boil. Stir in the couscous and remove from heat. Let stand 5 minutes. Stir in the pine nuts and lemon juice. Season with salt and pepper to taste.

1   tablespoon unsalted butter
½   small onion, minced
½   medium carrot, diced
1   cup chicken stock
¼   cup dark raisins, plumped
½   cup couscous
2   tablespoons pine nuts, toasted
    Juice of ½ lemon
    Salt and freshly ground black pepper to taste

springtime salad of pine nuts and avocados

light and good

While Rob and Suzie claim that "if we had any more 'aphrodisiac powers' in our life, we'd have trouble keeping our jobs," they nonetheless report that this springtime salad of pine nuts and avocados offers a "veritable symphony of textures – every taste bud on the tongue was aroused." *[Update: "If I'd known it was going to be this good, I would've bypassed that first marriage all together," says Rob. Married now for 18 years, Rob and Suzie are enjoying their new-found status as empty-nesters to explore new foods. Their latest cravings center around dim sum ("so tactile") and curries ("the depths, the layers, of flavors"). "I can see why India has a population problem," says Rob. At home, they still enjoy the simplicity of this salad.]*

YIELDS 2 TO 3 SERVINGS

To make the vinaigrette, combine the mustard, salt, pepper, honey, and vinegar with a whisk in a large serving bowl. Drizzle in the olive oil a little bit at a time, whisking until emulsified.

Tear the lettuce into bite-size pieces and add to the serving bowl. Toss with the dressing. Divide the lettuce between the serving plates. Sprinkle with the avocado, green onion, and pine nuts. Serve immediately.

2   teaspoons Dijon mustard
    Salt and freshly ground black pepper to taste
½   teaspoon honey
2   teaspoons white wine vinegar
2   tablespoons extra-virgin olive oil
1   head butterhead or Boston lettuce, cored
1   small avocado, peeled and chopped
1   green onion, thinly sliced
2   tablespoons pine nuts, toasted

pine nut muhammara

an addictive turkish red pepper dip

3   red bell peppers, roasted
    or 1 (16-ounce) jar, drained

1   (8-inch) piece of day-old
    baguette, crusts removed

½   cup pine nuts, toasted

2 to 3 cloves garlic, coarsely
    chopped

    Salt and freshly ground
    black pepper to taste

1   tablespoon freshly squeezed
    lemon juice

1 to 2 tablespoons pomegranate
    molasses (or unsulfured
    molasses if pomegranate
    is unavailable), divided

2   tablespoons extra-virgin
    olive oil, or more if desired

1 to 2 small Thai dried chiles
    (optional), seeded and
    minced

1   tablespoon chopped fresh
    parsley or cilantro for color

"Danny and I roasted the red bell peppers directly on the gas stovetop. Watching the shiny red peppers begin to blister and char was hypnotizing, and the resulting aromas – smoky, sophisticated, sultry – had me daydreaming of a honeymoon in the Mediterranean. Cleaning the charred skin off of the peppers revealed a smooth, bright, and flavorful flesh. We kept a watchful eye on each other so we didn't snack away at our prized ingredient, but of course, rules are meant to be broken."
Anneliese and Danny, Atlanta, GA

"Peeling red peppers is such a sensual experience. I recommend doing this one together – naked and blindfolded. It didn't take long before the line was blurred between lover and food."
Jeff and Donna, newlyweds, San Francisco, CA

As you can see from the testers' comments, freshly roasted bell peppers win high marks in the aphrodisiac category. Nevertheless, you can use a canned, store-bought version if you prefer to spend a little less time cooking and a little more time lovin'. Both versions work well, but the result tastes quite different. Either way, this dip tastes wonderful on oven-toasted pita bread, grilled fish, or a sandwich spread for smoky meats and peppery greens.

YIELDS ABOUT 2 1/2 CUPS

If using fresh red bell peppers, place them directly over a gas flame on the stove, turning frequently with tongs until charred on all sides. Place in a paper or plastic bag and let steam for 15 minutes. Rub off as much of the charred skin as possible with your hands. Slice the peppers open, remove the seeds, and coarsely chop the flesh.

Cut the baguette into large cubes. Place in a food processor, and pulse to create about ½ cup of breadcrumbs. Add the pine nuts and garlic, and pulse to grind into a paste. Season with salt and pepper. Add the roasted peppers, lemon juice, and 1 tablespoon of the molasses, and pulse until quite smooth. With the motor running, slowly pour in the olive oil until emulsified.

Taste and adjust the seasonings if necessary. If you prefer a thinner dip, drizzle in bit of water with the motor running to thin slightly. If you'd like a bit of heat, add the Thai chile, little by little, until your desired heat index is reached. For a sweeter dip, add the remaining molasses. Garnish with parsley or cilantro, and serve with grilled pita bread or raw vegetables.

shortbread cookies
with pine nuts

buttery happiness

Shortbread cookies' plainness is a virtue. They're the essential naked cookie. Pine nuts' delicate flavor (slightly more pronounced in imported Chinese pine nuts than in the domestic variety) makes them the perfect topping, since their subtle nuttiness doesn't compete with the taste of the cookies themselves and their pale golden color continues with the shortbread's monochromatic theme.

Nate and Keyana, together 10 months in London, England, took the naked cookie concept one step further: "We decided to add another twist of sensuality to our aphrodisiac shortbread by imposing a naked dress code. Sitting on the over-stuffed couch, we fed each other pieces of the dense, mildly sweet cookie, allowing the soft tang of the pine nuts to roll around our mouths. Yet despite the cookies' decadent taste and texture, we both felt nothing more than pleasantly full. Giving him a light kiss on the nose, I smiled, and admitted that I felt nothing. He agreed, adding that he felt nothing more than slightly silly. We each grinned a sheepish grin, each a little abashed at our earnest faith. We shared a chuckle. Moments later, we were lost in a tangle of naked arms, legs, and lips, true believers."

"These cookies brought us back to the first summer we spent apart after graduating from college. I was in the city, writing. Jim was in Maine, spending his days chasing after kids as a camp counselor. We racked up a lot of phone time that summer. On Sundays, he'd talk while I mixed up the dough for his cinnamon-spiced butter cookies. Like clockwork, four days later, I'd talk while he munched on that latest batch." *Kelli and Jim, dating 3 years, co-habitating for 1, New York City, NY*

½ cup (1 stick) unsalted butter, softened

¼ cup sugar

½ teaspoon vanilla extract

1 cup unbleached flour

¼ teaspoon salt

1 teaspoon ground cinnamon or nutmeg (optional)

½ cup Chinese pine nuts

YIELDS 12 COOKIES

Preheat the oven to 350 degrees. Cream together the butter, sugar, and vanilla in a medium-size mixing bowl until fluffy. Add the flour, salt, and cinnamon (if desired), and mix with a dough cutter or fork until a soft dough forms. Divide the dough in half and mound the halves on an ungreased baking sheet. Pat each into a round about 5 inches in diameter. Smooth out the edges with your fingers, and lightly prick the dough all over with a fork. Sprinkle the pine nuts on top of the rounds and press them into the dough. Use a fork to score each round into 6 wedges. Bake until the edges of the rounds are golden and the pine nuts are toasted, about 25 minutes. Let the rounds cool on the baking sheet, then break apart along the score-lines.

a v o c a d o

Once again, the Doctrine of Signatures is working in full force here. The modest avocado, with its bumpy, often lizard-like skin, peels away to reveal a creamy, natural butter. Cut in half, the pear-shaped symmetry of the avocado mimics the soft, buttery curves of a woman. A striking green that earned its own name in a box of crayons, the meat of the avocado gives under the pressure of a finger and melts on the tongue in a taste all its own. • In the Aztec culture, avocados were called *ahuacatl*, or testicle, and deemed so powerful that, as Cynthia Watson states, "(they) forbade village maidens to set one virginal toe outside the house while the fruit was being gathered." Today, avocados run the gamut of dishes and cuisines, and more importantly, virgins now have easy access to this forbidden fruit. • The Avocado. It's not just for guacamole anymore.

avocado chutney

zippy precursor to dinner

- 1 large ripe avocado
- 1 cup whole kernel corn, preferably fresh
- 1 small onion, finely chopped
- 1 red bell pepper, finely chopped
- ¼ cup olive oil
- 4 cloves garlic, minced
  Juice of 1 lime
- 2 teaspoons ground cumin
- 1 teaspoon chile powder
- 2 tablespoons chopped fresh oregano
- 1 tablespoon chopped fresh cilantro
  Salt and freshly ground black pepper to taste

I prepared this salsa as an appetizer for a modest fiesta at one couple's home. After 30 minutes of cerveza and salsa before dinner, Debbie gave us the requisite grand tour of their home. As we walked into their bedroom, Debbie motioned to the bed and, knowing of the aphrodisiacs on the menu, commented, "the workbench should be getting some use tonight." The true outcome of this story will always remain a mystery to all but Debbie, Jason, and their trusty workbench. *[Update: Debbie and Jason have their same, trusty workbench, but in a beautiful new home where they'll likely retire. Debbie does not allow chips in the bed, but swears that any other activities are fair game. They're about to celebrate their 34th anniversary. Since InterCourses' first release, their children have finished high school and college, and they've become grandparents to a little girl named Emma. The predictable cycle of life continues, but in a very good way.]*

YIELDS 4 SERVINGS

Slice the avocado in half. Remove the pit and scoop out the flesh into a mixing bowl. Coarsely mash the avocado, and then add the remaining ingredients and mix well. Cover and chill for up to 3 days. Serve with tortilla chips or grilled meats.

sun-dried tomato and avocado fettuccine

where cuba meets italy

- ¾ pound bowtie pasta
- 1 tablespoon olive oil
- ¼ cup diced sun-dried tomatoes
- 1 tablespoon sherry wine vinegar
  Juice of 1 lime
- ¼ cup julienned fresh basil
- 1 tablespoon chopped green onions
- 2 tablespoons diced green bell pepper
- 1 tablespoon chopped walnuts
- 2 tablespoons minced fresh cilantro
- 1 small avocado, diced
  Salt and freshly ground black pepper to taste
- ½ pound bacon, cooked and crumbled

Chris and Pat share an apartment in Austin, Texas. Under certain conditions, though, their relationship has been known to cross over that understood roommate barrier into a more, shall we say, romantic arena. Such was the case with their dinner of sun-dried tomato and avocado fettuccine. According to Chris, "I fixed up a pot of this pasta and, as usual, asked Pat to join me. We usually eat in my room – the window unit's better in there, and my T.V. has a remote. We sat Indian-style on the bed, clicked on *Lois and Clarke*, and ate our pasta. He spent the night in my room. What can I say?"

YIELDS 2 TO 3 SERVINGS

Bring a large pot of salted water to boil over high heat. Cook the pasta according to package directions, or until al dente.

While the pasta is cooking, combine the olive oil, sun-dried tomatoes, vinegar, lime juice, basil, green onions, green pepper, walnuts, cilantro, avocado, and bacon in a large bowl. Toss well. Drain the pasta and toss with the avocado mixture. Serve hot, at room temperature, or chilled as a pasta salad.

"It seems to me that the anticipation of an aphrodisiac meal is oftentimes aphrodisiac enough. My significant other and I couldn't stop smiling and casting knowing glances at each other the whole time we were preparing the meal."

Karen and Rick, happily dating 6 months, NYC

hot black bean
and avocado torta

one extremely reliable sandwich

1   (12-inch) baguette,
    cut in half

½   cup mashed black beans

½   pound thickly sliced ham

1   tomato, sliced

1   tablespoon mayonnaise

½   avocado, thinly sliced

⅓   pound Oaxacan string
    cheese, sliced

    Juice of 1 lime

1   tablespoon chopped
    fresh cilantro

Every Monday, Wednesday, and Friday. Like clockwork, I would meet Kimber and Amy at Bar El Jardin, our favorite open-air cafe in the zocalo of Oaxaca. We all three ordered the same thing. Every single time. And we never tired of it. Jambon torta y una lemonada, por favor. We would sit at our table under our umbrella and eat and drink and laugh and flirt with boys who passed by. This is how we found our dates for salsa dancing, and we wouldn't have traded our method for anything in the world. [*Update: Amy has returned to Oaxaca four times, lured still by its utter captivating-ness. "I took my husband after we married, and he fell in love with it right away," she says. Most recently, she went with her mother and sisters for a week of cooking classes. They made mango sorbet, green salsa in a molcajete, stuffed squash blossoms, and all sorts of delectable treats. The minute she got home, she made her husband the chiles en nogada, stuffed poblanos with pork, fruits, and nuts in a walnut cream sauce. "Yep, I wooed him with that one!" she says. No doubt she'll be going back again to further expand her repertoire of culinary seduction.*]

YIELDS 2 SERVINGS

Preheat the oven to 350 degrees. Slice each baguette in half lengthwise, then warm until toasty. Heat the black beans in the microwave or a small saucepan until warmed through. Sauté the ham and tomato slices in a skillet until the ham browns slightly and the tomato warms through.

To assemble the torta, spread the top half of the baguette with some of the mashed black beans. On the bottom half, spread with mayonnaise and then layer the ham, tomatoes, cheese, and avocado. Squirt with some fresh lime juice and sprinkle with the chopped cilantro. Top with the black-bean half, and enjoy your torta with a glass of fresh lemonade made from sparkling water, lemon juice, sugar, and lots and lots of ice.

grilled red snapper with avocado sauce

horseradish gives this sauce a kick

This recipe can be prepared with other types of fish, but for my sake, please use red snapper. Red snapper takes me back to a beach in Puerto Escondido, an untouristy, beautiful stretch of sand, rocks, and waves on the Pacific side of southern Mexico. Sun-burned and tired, we stumbled onto this open-air restaurant on the quieter end of the beach. Each of us ordered the snapper – it was prepared simply, just a whole fish grilled with lemon and cilantro. We were living a postcard that night with the palm trees and hammocks swaying around us, and the salty air brushing against our lips. All to say, you may borrow this memory as garnish for your grilled red snapper with avocado sauce.

YIELDS 2 SERVINGS

Combine the fillets and wine in a shallow dish. Marinate in the refrigerator for no more than 30 minutes.

Prepare a hot grill. Remove the snapper from the marinade and pat dry. Rub 1 tablespoon of the butter on both sides of the fillets. Sprinkle with the paprika. Grill 4 to 5 minutes, or until just cooked through.

Alternatively, set a large skillet over medium heat and add the butter. Cook the fish until golden brown on each side, turning once.

To make the sauce, place a large skillet over medium-high heat and add the remaining tablespoon of butter. Sauté the onion until translucent. Whisk in the flour and salt, and cook until the flour begins to turn a very light brown. Whisk in the hot water, stirring constantly to dissolve any lumps.

Remove the skillet from the heat. Stir in the sour cream, horseradish, and avocado. Reduce the heat to low, and return the skillet to the burner. Warm until just heated through and then spoon over the fillets. Sprinkle with lime juice and cilantro.

2 red snapper fillets, pin bones removed

½ cup white wine

2 tablespoons unsalted butter, softened

1 teaspoon paprika

2 tablespoons minced onion

1 tablespoon flour

¼ teaspoon seasoned salt

½ cup hot water

¼ cup sour cream

1 tablespoon horseradish

1 small ripe avocado, diced

1 lime, quartered, or 2 key limes, halved

1 tablespoon minced fresh cilantro

l i b a t i o n s

"Behold how Bacchus, the aider and abettor of Venus, doth offer himself . . . let us therefore drink up this wine, that we may do utterly away with the cowardice of shame and get us the courage of pleasure." Apuleius, *The Golden Ass*, as quoted in *Secrets of Venus*.

Alcohol has served throughout history as the basis for most love potions, masking foul tastes of bizarre ingredients. Today, fortunately, we typically rely on alcohol not for its hocus-pocus concoctions of wormwood, but for its innate aphrodisiacal powers alone. After a mere drink or two, it lowers inhibitions and allows people to do what they only fantasized as a possibility just one hour before. Whether sipping margaritas on the beach, savoring a glass of Merlot with some Camembert, or shooting body shots in a game of quarters, alcohol pushes aside the doubts, fears, and mores that typically restrain people from pursuing what might have been. With a few sips of alcohol, they might just get to find out. Here's a toast to going for it.

champagne terrine
blissfully light

4 gelatin leaves or 1 packet Knox Gelatine

3 large grapefruit

3 oranges

½ pint fresh raspberries or 1 cup frozen

¾ cup orange juice

¼ cup sugar

¾ cup Champagne

2 tablespoons Grand Marnier

This recipe, graciously shared by Chef José Gutierrez of The Peabody Hotel in Memphis, TN, will make your lover very happy. Unendingly talented, José sees to it that each dish he creates is a memorable one. Champagne terrines not excluded. [*Update: José's all about new things these days. He's left his longtime post at the Peabody to open a hot new restaurant called Encore with his fiancée, Colleen. Together, they share a 24/7 passion for food. "We are consumed by food," says José, "and it's integral to who we are as a couple." The menu at Encore benefits from this overlapping of work + love + life, providing customers with a passion they can, most literally, taste.*]

YIELDS 4 SERVINGS

If using gelatin leaves, soak for 1½ hours in cold water. To prepare the grapefruit and oranges, place one fruit on a cutting board and slice off the bottom and the top of the fruit so it will sit flat on the board. Using a sharp knife, carefully cut away the peel and pith, leaving as much of the flesh as possible. Take the peeled fruit in your hand and slice in between each membrane so the flesh slips out. Repeat with the remaining grapefruit and oranges, reserving any juice.

Layer the grapefruit sections, orange sections, and fresh or frozen raspberries neatly in a terrine or loaf pan. Warm the orange juice, any reserved juices from the fruits, and the sugar in a small saucepan over medium heat, stirring to dissolve the sugar. Add the gelatin leaves and cook until completely melted. Add the Champagne and Grand Marnier, and then pour over the terrine. Cover and refrigerate at least 4 hours before serving.

Alternatively, if using the Knox Gelatine, sprinkle the powder into ½ cup of the orange juice and let stand 10 minutes. Warm the remaining ¼ cup of orange juice and sugar, stirring to dissolve. Pour in the Knox mixture and stir to completely melt the gelatin. Continue with the rest of the recipe as directed.

champagne laced with raspberry

Champagne. Baci. Imported cheese. Raspberries. Saturday afternoon, in bed. According to Aaron, "It was, without a doubt, the most sensual experience I've ever had. She fed me. She watched me. She kissed me. She drank me with her eyes, savoring me like she did each bubble of the Möet White Star, each morsel of the chocolatey-hazelnut Baci, each wedge of the creamy cheese, each delicate raspberry she held between her lips. I felt her effect on every inch of my body, and I wanted to taste her, sip her, just as I had the chilled champagne with raspberry." *[Update: "Okay, yes, that was an amazing experience," says Aaron. "It sounds so over-the-top now, but that's really what it's like at the beginning of a relationship, right? It has to be, otherwise we'd never get to the stages beyond that. I'm happily married now, though not to this girl. My wife and I had some similarly erotic food experiences at the beginning of our relationship. Now she seems to get more turned on when I do the dishes. Whatever works, I say."]*

1 teaspoon framboise

1 teaspoon kirsch

8 ounces chilled extra-dry Champagne

Fresh raspberries for garnish

YIELDS 2 SERVINGS

Pour half the framboise and half the kirsch into 2 chilled Champagne glasses. Tilt glasses to coat. Add the Champagne and top with 1 or 2 raspberries.

lemon-honey spritzer

"David and I decided to test this recipe on a Thursday night. While he mixed everything together, I pulled some chairs out into the front lawn, moved the stereo to the screen door, put in some Harry Connick, and invited our dogs Rip and Rem out to join us. We just sat, relaxing and sipping, while the street lights changed their shades of colors and the dogs chased the occasional firefly and the crickets chirped around us." *Terry, reminiscing on a summer night with David and lemon-honey spritzers, together 4 years, Shreveport, LA*

½ (6-ounce) can frozen lemonade concentrate, thawed

4 tablespoons Grand Marnier

4 tablespoons honey, warmed

1 (750-milliliter) bottle Champagne, chilled

Fresh strawberries, hulled and sliced

YIELDS 4 TO 5 SERVINGS

Combine the lemonade and Grand Marnier in a pitcher. Add the honey, stirring until dissolved, and then chill. When ready to serve, pop open the Champagne and combine with the lemonade mixture. Pour into flutes and garnish with strawberry slices.

"Your stature is like that of the palm, and your breasts

like clusters of fruit. I said, 'I will climb the palm tree;

I will take hold of its fruit.' May your breasts be like the

clusters of the vine, the fragrance of your breath like

apples, and your mouth like the best wine." "May the wine

go straight to my lover, flowing gently over lips and teeth.

I belong to my lover, and his desire is for me." Song of Songs 7:7-10

mint-chocolate smoothie

chocolate mint ice cream grows up

Thomas and Patty, officially together for three weeks in Houston, TX, tested this recipe because Thomas had a new espresso machine he wanted to try out. After tearing him away from the frother (an exciting mechanism for any new espresso machine owner), Patty was able to turn his concentration toward this creamy drink by uttering just one simple phrase: "Hon, aphrodisiacs, remember?" Try it – it'll probably work – even for a man with a new toy.

YIELDS 2 SERVINGS

Coarsely chop the chocolate. Place all but 1 to 2 tablespoons in the blender. Finely chop the remaining chocolate for garnish.

Add the ice, milk, crème de menthe, and coffee to the blender. Process until completely smooth. Serve in chilled glasses and garnish with the remaining chocolate and a sprig of mint.

8 ounces high-quality dark chocolate, preferably mint flavored

½ cup crushed ice

1 cup milk

½ teaspoon crème de menthe

½ cup coffee

Fresh mint sprigs for garnish

the little death by chocolate

an amazing hot cocoa

This cockle-warming libation is the very definition of sinful. It will knock you and your partner's socks off (at the very least).

YIELDS 2 SERVINGS

To make the whipped cream, combine the cocoa powder, sugar, and 2 teaspoons of the cream in a small bowl, and stir to a smooth paste. Pour the rest of the cream into a medium-size mixing bowl, add the cocoa mixture and the vanilla, and whip until stiff peaks form. Refrigerate until ready to use.

To make the hot chocolate, combine the cocoa powder, sugar, and water in a small bowl, and stir until a smooth paste forms. Heat the milk in a small saucepan until it steams; do not boil. Add the cocoa paste to the hot milk and stir until thoroughly incorporated.

Pour 1½ ounces of Godiva liqueur into each of two large, warmed coffee mugs. Fill each mug three-quarters full with hot chocolate, and top each with an extremely generous helping of chocolate whipped cream.

for the whipped cream:

1 tablespoon Scharffen Berger unsweetened cocoa powder

1 tablespoon sugar

1 cup heavy whipping cream, chilled, divided

½ teaspoon vanilla extract

for the hot chocolate:

6 tablespoons Scharffen Berger unsweetened cocoa powder

2 tablespoons sugar

6 tablespoons water

1½ to 2 cups whole milk

3 ounces Godiva liqueur

jamaican fruit salsa

come . . . to the islands

for the fruit salsa:

- ⅓ cup dark rum
- 3 tablespoons coconut-flavored rum
- ⅓ cup rumrunner mix
- ½ cup pineapple juice
- 1 pint fresh strawberries,* hulled and sliced in half, divided
- 2 bananas, chopped, divided
- 1 cup diced pineapple
- 1 cup fresh blueberries* (about ½ pint)
- 1 cup fresh blackberries* (about ½ pint)
- 2 sprigs fresh mint

for the whipped cream :

- 1 cup (½ pint) heavy whipping cream, chilled
- 1 tablespoon superfine sugar
- ½ teaspoon vanilla extract

According to Jen of the Jen/Henry combo, "One of the few things I remember hearing from the Ghandi of '90s love, John Gray of the Venus/Mars combo, is that the best foreplay is in the mind. It should start with a sexy intimation in the morning and fester all day until you get the chance to act out your incubating fantasies with your partner." Says Jen, "Be sure to prepare this salsa at least two days before the date. The flavors need the time to infuse, and just seeing it in the fridge every time I opened it was enough foreplay for any woman."

YIELDS 6 TO 8 SERVINGS

Combine the rums, rumrunner mix, pineapple juice, and half of the strawberries in a non-reactive mixing bowl. Combine the remaining strawberries and half the banana in a blender and purée. Add to the rum mixture. Stir in the remaining banana, along with the pineapple, blueberries, blackberries, and mint sprigs; gently combine. Cover and refrigerate for 2 hours, and then remove the mint sprigs. (The salsa can be stored in the refrigerator for up to 2 days without the mint.)

If serving with whipped cream, whip the cream in a large mixing bowl with an electric mixer or whisk until the cream begins to thicken. Add the sugar and vanilla, and continue beating until soft peaks form. Be careful not to overbeat, or the cream will begin to separate and curdle.

Serve with small wedges of toasted angel food cake or shortbread cookies. Garnish with whipped cream, if desired, and fresh mint leaves.

* If fresh berries aren't in season, you can use frozen fruits. Thaw first in the refrigerator.

wine-soaked cherries
and pears over pound cake

warm and sensuous

Though not specifically covered in this book, cherries and pears have an abundance of aphrodisiacal qualities all their own, a fact all too apparent in wine-soaked cherries and pears over pound cake. The warm, succulent fruit saturated with wine will elicit a heartfelt "Oh!," the sweet, melting cream will conjure up images of The Promised Land, and all will be yours tonight and forevermore.

Y I E L D S   2   T O   4   S E R V I N G S

Combine the wine, sugar, and lemon zest in a medium saucepan. Set over medium heat and stir until the sugar dissolves. Stir in the cherries. Bring to a boil, reduce the heat, and simmer for 10 minutes. Stir in the pears, if desired, and simmer for 5 minutes more.

While the fruits are poaching, spread the pound cake with butter and toast to a golden brown. Whip the cream in a large mixing bowl with an electric mixer or whisk until it begins to thicken. Add the sugar and vanilla, and continue beating until soft peaks form. Be careful not to overbeat, as the cream will be begin to curdle and separate.

Generously spoon the fruit and juices over the cake. Serve warm, topped with a dollop of cream.

½ cup red wine (the better the wine, the better the dish)

½ cup sugar

Zest of ½ lemon

¾ pound cherries, pitted

2 pears (optional), peeled and cut into uniform cubes

4 thick slices pound cake

1 tablespoon unsalted butter, softened

½ cup heavy whipping cream, chilled

½ tablespoon superfine sugar

¼ teaspoon vanilla extract

bittersweet

take it slow

Cynar is an Italian apéritif made from, of all things, artichokes. By itself, it's too bitter for many people's taste. Add a cube of raw Demerara sugar, however, and you strike a perfect balance between the bitter and the sweet.

"The unusual bitter flavor completely coated the top of my tongue with each sip, making everything about my wife taste that much sweeter when we finished." *Jack and Madge, married 3 years, Santa Cruz, CA*

Y I E L D S   1   S E R V I N G

Rim a rocks glass with the orange wedge. (Discard the wedge.) Add three or four ice cubes to the glass, pour in the Cynar, drop in the sugar cube, and stir briefly. Top with a splash of soda and garnish with the orange slice. Add another sugar cube, if desired.

1 small wedge of orange

2 ounces (¼ cup) Cynar

1 cube Demerara or other raw brown sugar, or more if desired

Soda or seltzer

1 slice orange

iced coffee "43"

puts your standard, workaday coffee to shame

6   ounces (¾ cup) brewed
    dark-roast coffee, chilled

1 to 1½ ounces
    (2 to 3 tablespoons)
    Cuarenta Y Tres
    ("43") liqueur

1   ounce (2 tablespoons)
    heavy cream

Consider having one of these iced coffees before getting down to work (so to speak). But don't have two – cause then you'll be eighty-sixed. (The Spanish butterscotch-flavored liqueur Cuarenta Y Tres is, by the way, sold at most liquor stores.) To keep it sober – but why would you want to do anything like that? – combine the chilled coffee with sweetened condensed milk and drizzle in a spoon of caramel syrup.

"It's close to 100 degrees outside and humid – one of those lazy afternoons where the best thing for a person to do is sit in front of a fan and try to breathe. I bring out the coffee for me and him – extra ice and extra strong. The cool condensation on the outside of the glass tempts my parched throat, so I lick the glass.

"He glances over at me and takes a sip, cream still clinging to his upper lip as he puts his glass down. All I wanted to do was to suck that cooled cream off his lip, and I told him so.

"We spent the rest of the afternoon in the bedroom – where it's air-conditioned." *Kelly and Pat, together 3 years, Toronto, ON, Canada*

"It feels great when you drink it . . . so smooth and so silky." *Janey, who started the chase with Rick in 1969 and captured him for good in 1970, El Dorado, AR*

YIELDS 1 SERVING

Fill a tall glass with ice cubes. Add the coffee and Cuarenta Y Tres and stir briefly. Float the heavy cream on top. In this case, "float the cream" merely means to spoon the cream gently on top, without stirring. It will gradually descend through the coffee for a slightly more dramatic effect, visually and taste-wise.

goldfinger

This lascivious Champagne cocktail requires a simple honey syrup. To make it, combine equal parts honey and water in a saucepan and set over medium heat, stirring occasionally to ensure that the honey dissolves completely. Just as the solution reaches a boil, remove the pan from the heat and let cool completely before using. Or, combine in a microwave-safe bowl and microwave just until the mixture begins to bubble. When making this (or any other) Champagne cocktail, be sure to place all the other ingredients in the flute before adding the Champagne.

"If you had asked me three years ago, I would have told you that I didn't believe in love at first sight and I didn't believe that aphrodisiacs truly worked. Then I saw the man that would become my husband a year later. When I saw him, the world stopped and I felt for the first time that everything was connected and something brought me to that place at that time; I fell in love at first sight. Then, almost three years later, I had my first sip of this Champagne cocktail with my husband and felt again like everything was connected, but this time it was the honey and the bubbly coming together, a marrying of flavors and the senses instead of people. Now, I believe that aphrodisiacs truly work."
Kimberly and Mike, married 2 years, Memphis, TN

"Well, as a newlywed with Baptist tendencies, this whole aphrodisiac thing felt a little scandalous – especially when you add alcohol to the equation. My wife and I tried this one early in the morning and late at night. I'd say that it's far better suited for late night seductions – it's just too powerful for an a.m. release. I can say, however, that two servings in the morning did get us through our first round of financial discussions and bill payments without too much of a fuss. The evening test was much more interesting, but a good Southern Baptist never kisses and tells. You'll just have to imagine. King Solomon would be proud." *Jeff and Dana, married 2 months, San Francisco, CA*

1 twist of lemon

½ ounce (1 tablespoon) cognac

1 teaspoon simple honey syrup

2 dashes orange bitters

5 ounces (about ⅔ cup) brut Champagne, chilled

YIELDS 1 SERVING

Rim a Champagne flute with the lemon twist and drop the twist into the glass. Add the cognac, honey syrup, and bitters. Gently top with Champagne.

f i g s

If you've never had a fig before, it will not — cannot — taste, smell, look, or feel as you imagined it would — because a ripe fig tastes sweeter than any dried nugget of trail-mix fig, and a plump one smells gentler than any hyper-syruped canned version. • A small, pear-shaped delicacy, its skin ranges from a soft white to a purpley-black, its flesh from a yellowish-pink to a vibrant pinkish-red. • And its feel, oh its feel. A knife slices through the fresh fruit like soft butter. The tiny, edible seeds seem unending, weaving layer upon layer of texture and flavor. All ridges work inward to a core, painting a relief portrait of the soft world of the inner thighs. When you eat a fig, you are tasting history, Cleopatra, Dionysian orgies, the Roman Saturnalia. And when its juice runs over your tongue, you are drinking pure, unadulterated sensuality.

fig chutney

a bold taste of exotica

¼ cup dried figs, chopped

¼ cup dried cherries

¼ cup dried cranberries

¼ cup dried apricots, chopped

¼ cup dried peaches, chopped

¼ cup raisins

½ small onion, finely diced

2 tablespoons cider vinegar

⅛ cup pistachios, toasted

⅛ cup almonds, toasted

½ tablespoon minced fresh ginger

½ teaspoon minced green chile pepper

 Salt and freshly ground black pepper to taste

2 tablespoons freshly squeezed lemon juice (about ½ lemon)

"In our early years of marriage, we lived in a little white house with two ceiling fans and no air conditioner. But in our front yard alone, we had all kinds of fruit trees. Being parents of three children and living on a limited budget of $10,000 per year, we made use of every edible piece of fruit our trees produced. We ate it fresh, canned, candied, baked, fried. And later in the year, when we'd long since used up all the fresh and were running low on the children's favorite − canned preserves − Bud and I would turn to our dried fruit to make a version of this dip. After putting the kids to bed, we moved on to the screened porch where our 12-year-old parrot stayed (and talked incessantly), and reflected on the day's events over fig chutney and homemade ginger-ale." *Bud and Rowena, married 44 years, Vicksburg, MS*

YIELDS 12 SERVINGS

Combine the figs, cherries, cranberries, apricots, peaches, raisins, onion, and vinegar in a medium saucepan. Add enough water to cover and bring to a boil. Reduce the heat and simmer for 15 to 20 minutes, or until the sauce becomes syrupy, stirring frequently.

Purée the pistachios, almonds, ginger, chile pepper, salt, and pepper in a food processor. (Or mash with a mortar and pestle.) Add the lemon juice and the nut mixture to the fruits, and stir to combine. Place in a container with a tight-fitting lid. Refrigerate for up to 2 weeks.

This chutney goes well any variety of ways, but particularly so with pork or lamb shish kebabs over basmati rice.

creamy stuffed figs

crème de dieu

"I have to admit that I didn't believe in the powers of aphrodisiacs, especially when we began to fight in the middle of testing the recipes. Things can get pretty tense in his kitchen – he tends to be very critical when it comes to that sacred part of his house. I prepared the dessert and appetizer first while he chopped and sautéed his way through the entrée. Tensions arose when he began to complain about the way I cut this, the pan I put that in, etc. . . . I guess I'd just had enough, because after one too many 'No, you're supposed to fold it in, not whisk it in,' I just dunked my hand in the cream cheese and smeared it across his face. A very bold move, I might add – it could've gone either way at that point. Fortunately, it went to playful fighting. Then playful licking. Then playful . . . okay, I'm drawing the line on my experience here. Suffice it to say, everything tasted good." *Becky, on her "friend" Norm, Jacksonville, FL [Update: Becky married someone else. Thank God. Norm was a jerk, but the husband's fabulous. She's finally getting all she deserves.]*

YIELDS 2 SERVINGS

- 4 ounces pancetta or lean bacon, cooked and chopped
- ½ cup cream cheese
- 1 tablespoon chopped chives
  Salt and freshly ground black pepper to taste
- 4 fresh figs, stems removed
- ¼ cup coarsely chopped walnuts, toasted

Set a skillet over medium heat and cook the pancetta until cooked through and crisped. Drain and chop into small pieces.

Combine the pancetta, cream cheese, chives, salt, and pepper in a bowl. Make 2 vertical slices in each fig and spread into 4 quarters. Fill with a generous spoonful of the cream cheese mixture and sprinkle with the walnuts. Eat.

fruits in white wine

succulently mingled textures

"Laura and I have been together for more than half of our lives. It takes us by surprise sometimes. She's always had a wonderful hand in her kitchen, but sometimes I like to surprise her with a treat. This dish was a perfect combination of two of her favorites – white wine and lush fruits – and perfect for me because it is so simple." *Jim, on a perfect dessert and his perfect Laura, married 32 years, Charleston, SC*

YIELDS 4 SERVINGS

- ½ cup sweet white wine
- 1 tablespoon sugar
- 4 figs, quartered
- 2 apricots, peeled and quartered
- 2 plums, chopped
- 2 nectarines, peeled and chopped
- 2 tablespoons coarsely chopped walnuts

Mix the wine and sugar, stirring until the sugar dissolves. Add the fruit and toss. Refrigerate, covered, for 1 hour or longer to let flavors meld. Sprinkle with the walnuts before serving.

FOOD COMES FIRST, THEN MORALS.

Bertolt Brecht, *Die Dreigroschenoper (Threepenny Opera)*, 1928, Act 2, Scene 3

honey-drenched figs

w a r m   j u i c y   d r i p p y   s t i c k y

Ineffably decadent. Use only with experienced lovers.

Y I E L D S   2   S E R V I N G S

Grill the figs over a low heat until heated through, turning occasionally. Warm the honey.

Place the figs on individual serving plates and drizzle with enough honey to coat lightly.

Top with a bit of crème fraîche, if desired, and sprinkle with the pecans. Enjoy while still warm.

8   figs, cut in half lengthwise

¼   cup honey

¼   cup crème fraîche (optional)

3   tablespoons finely chopped pecans

fresh figs
sautéed in butter

a   l o v e l y   a d d i t i o n   t o   r o a s t e d   m e a t s

"I served this dish as a quick appetizer before dinner. We ate it standing up in the kitchen. I served half savory for my palate (sea salt and freshly cracked pepper only) and half sweet for my sweetheart (served with a few tablespoons of heavy whipping cream). As we stood in the kitchen, side by side, sharing a fork, tasting each presentation, I was reminded of why I fell in love with this man so many years ago." *Lisa and Jeff, together 8 years, Bedford, TX*

2   tablespoons unsalted butter

6 to 8 fresh figs, cut in half lengthwise

Salt and freshly ground black pepper

Y I E L D S   3   T O   4   S E R V I N G S

Set a large sauté pan over medium heat. Melt the butter and add the figs, cut-side down, in one layer. Sauté for 2 to 3 minutes, or until slightly golden. Carefully turn the figs over and continue cooking another minute or so. Season with salt and pepper, and serve immediately as a side to a slice of Maytag blue or roasted game, or with a spoon of chilled cream for dessert.

sausage with fig sauce

spicy flavors tempered with natural sweetness

for the fig sauce:

½ cup sugar

½ cup red wine vinegar

½ stick cinnamon

2 cloves

1 teaspoon freshly
   grated nutmeg

½ slice lemon

1 pound fresh or canned
   figs, drained

for the sausages:

¾ pound spicy Italian
   sausage links

2 teaspoons olive oil

3 tablespoons white wine

   Salt and freshly ground
   black pepper to taste

"The first meal we ever ate together was a late-night pizza. Not incredible, not exciting, not even on plates . . . maybe a little romantic. The first aphrodisiac meal we ever ate together was italian sausage with fig sauce on a bed of rice — on plates. Neither of us had ever eaten figs other than a Newton, and we weren't exactly sure of what to expect. And to be truthful, we were probably more than a little intimidated. But in the end, the actual swelling of the sauce-soaked figs brought only one thing to mind.

The flavors teetered between sweet and spicy. Something familiar and not so familiar, all at once. Each bite just a little different than the bite before. And like the introduction to a promising night, full of welcomed surprise. Just the idea of the meal created an incredible, uncontrollable excitement that carried over from the kitchen to the dining room into the bedroom. We're planning on many more aphrodisiac meals for the future." *Matthew and Kelly, together 2 years, Chicago, IL [Update: "After 12 years together, our old date night had become our new therapy night. We spent less time together. We ate more meals apart. And we only seemed to be able to talk to each other when Sally, MS LPC, was interpreting for one of us. So, we set the table for two. We decided to have our first aphrodisiac meal all over again. We prepared the meal together. We ate together. And we were quiet together. We were the kind of quiet that would normally make me uncomfortable. The kind of quiet that I had always wanted to find with someone. The kind of quiet that brings peace. So, where are we now: We're still in therapy together. We've christened another evening for our date nights. And we try to always eat dinner together."]*

YIELDS 2 TO 3 SERVINGS

For the fig sauce, combine the sugar, vinegar, cinnamon, cloves, nutmeg, and lemon in a saucepan. Bring to a boil over high heat. Reduce the heat and simmer for 5 minutes. Add the figs. Cook for 15 minutes, or until the syrup has reduced and thickened slightly. If possible, cool in the syrup overnight.

For the sausages, set a large skillet over medium to medium-high heat and add the oil. Add the sausages to the hot oil to brown. Pour in the wine, scraping the bottom of the pan to release any browned bits. Reduce the heat to medium-low, cover, and cook until the sausages are cooked through and the wine has evaporated. (If the sausages are starting to burn, add ½ to 1 cup of water and cook until all the water has evaporated.) Add the figs and their syrup to warm through. Season with salt and pepper to taste. Serve the sausages with the whole figs and spoon with the fig syrup.

chocolate fig bundles

one bundle alone will not satisfy

Cheryl enjoyed making these chocolate fig bundles. "My first experience with phyllo, but not intimidating at all – I loved spreading the butter over those sheets." Frank enjoyed eating them. "This is like the sweet nectar of the gods – chocolate, almonds, figs, butter, phyllo pastry. Bring it on!"

YIELDS 2 OR 3 SERVINGS

Slit the figs down the side. Place in a bowl with 1 tablespoon brandy; let stand for 30 minutes to plump with flavor.

Grind 10 of the almonds in a food processor with the granulated sugar or chop very finely by hand. Combine the ground almonds, sugar, chocolate, and remaining ½ tablespoon of brandy in a small bowl until it forms a paste. Stuff 1 teaspoon of the mixture into each fig along with 1 whole almond.

Preheat the oven to 375 degrees. Set a single phyllo sheet on a clean surface and keep the others moist with a damp kitchen towel. Lightly brush the sheet with melted butter. Fold the right third over the middle then the left third over the middle (you will have a 3-layer sheet). Lightly butter the surface and sprinkle with 2 teaspoons confectioners' sugar. Cut the strip in half to form 2 rectangles.

Place a stuffed fig, slit-side up, in the center of each rectangle. Pinch each corner in half, and bring each corner together in the center to form a star shape. Brush the fig packet with melted butter. Repeat the process with each fig and place the bundles on a baking sheet. Bake for 13 minutes, or until crisp and golden brown. Remove from the baking sheet to a wire rack and cool slightly.

Place 2 or 3 bundles on each dessert plate and sprinkle with confectioners' sugar.

6 dried figs

1½ tablespoons brandy, divided

16 whole almonds, toasted, divided

1 tablespoon sugar

½ ounce high-quality semisweet chocolate, finely chopped

3 sheets phyllo pastry, thawed

2 tablespoons unsalted butter, melted

3 tablespoons confectioners' sugar, plus more for garnish

braised beef short ribs with black mission figs

excessively good comfort food

I have been with my boyfriend for eight years, but I've never spent a Valentine's Day with him. Not a single one. That's my busy season, when I'm out telling everyone else how to have a happy Valentine's Day. I don't mind, because he's taught me how to have Valentine's many other days of the year. Still, I like for my February 14th to be nice, so I was thrilled when my friend Jason from high school was able to drive out from San Francisco and join me at a Valentine's event in Napa. After hours of talking to winery customers and standing on my feet, I couldn't wait to have a relaxing dinner. Only problem was, it was 10:00 p.m. on the busiest restaurant night of the year in an area of California where most things close by 6:00 p.m. We stumbled onto the Girl and the Fig, a restaurant I'd heard about for several years. We walked in, and they were packed. Every reservation was filled through closing. They must have recognized the tired look of defeat on our faces, because they sat us down on couches in the waiting area and brought us TV trays, silverware, and menus. There, we ate a four-course, primo Valentine's dinner, including Sondra's to-die-for short ribs with figs. This recipe will take some work for the home cook – and you best take your time browning those ribs, as that's what's going to give your dish the depth of flavor you want. But whoever said love was easy?

"Seriously, the aroma of this dish was the best part – after the taste, of course. And while we did go to two farmer's markets and two grocery stores to find the ingredients (don't search for figs when it's not fig season . . . just give in and go for the canned!), and it took a lot of work to prepare and cook, we had a fun time. It had been a while since we'd spent a weekend doing something together – they're usually spent washing laundry, running errands, and mowing the yard, which we usually split up and do separately. Maybe that's not as sexy, but after almost 10 years together, it was nice." *Brent and Nick, together 9 years, Kensington, MD*

"I served this dish at a dinner party thrown for the sole purpose of evaluating whether or not a certain guy had potential. When I saw him pick up a bone and start searching for a bit of marrow, I felt a sudden urge to ask all of my other guests to go home." *Gwyneth, Albuquerque, NM* (continued)

Combine all the marinade ingredients in an extra-large, resealable plastic bag or a large dish. Mix well. Add the ribs and coat well. Marinate in the refrigerator for at least 12 hours.

Tie the parsley, thyme, and bay leaf with kitchen twine to make a bouquet garni. Remove the ribs from the marinade and scrape off any excess marinade. Pat dry and season with salt and pepper to taste. Set a large, heavy Dutch oven or roasting pan over medium-high heat and add 2 tablespoons of oil. Sear the ribs in batches on every side until nicely browned, making sure the drippings don't burn. Deglaze the pan with ½ cup of water, scraping up any flavorful browned bits. Pour the deglazing liquid and bits into a small bowl and reserve. (If the drippings seem to be burning, remove the ribs immediately and deglaze the pan with a bit of water. Wipe out any burned pieces with a paper towel, reduce the heat, add more oil, and continue browning the ribs.)

Preheat the oven to 325 degrees. Add 2 tablespoons oil to the pan and adjust the heat to medium. Add the carrots, onions, and celery and cook until the vegetables are caramelized. Add the tomatoes and cook another 5 minutes. Pour in the red wine, stirring the bottom of the pan to release any browned bits. Add the seared ribs and reserved deglazing liquid, figs, and bouquet garni. Add enough stock to cover the ribs by 2 inches. Bring to a simmer. Cover and braise for 4 hours, turning the ribs every hour and skimming off excess fat. (If the sauce seems to be drying out, add more stock.) Remove the ribs, smother with the sauce, and serve with mashed potatoes or creamy polenta and a glass of Côtes du Rhône. (Please note, Gwyneth swears by the mashed potatoes. "Men go CRAZY for mashed potatoes.")

* You'll find lots of options online for demi-glace, an über-reduced sauce that you can reconstitute with water. It's an expensive alternative to canned stock, but offers premium flavor.

for the marinade:

3   tablespoons minced garlic

1   tablespoon salt, plus more to taste

1   tablespoon freshly ground black pepper, plus more to taste

1   tablespoon chopped fresh parsley

1   tablespoon chopped fresh thyme

½   cup red wine

½   cup extra-virgin olive oil

1   tablespoon sherry vinegar

for the braise:

6   beef short ribs, about 2 x 3-inches each

4   sprigs fresh parsley

2   sprigs fresh thyme

1   bay leaf
    Salt and freshly ground black pepper to taste

2 to 4 tablespoons grapeseed or vegetable oil

1   carrot, diced

2   medium onions, diced

3   stalks celery, diced

3   Roma tomatoes, roughly chopped

1   cup red wine

1   cup diced Black Mission Figs

6 to 10 cups veal stock, or chicken or beef stock*

resources

asian ingredients: If your pantry (and grocery store) are missing a few of the Asian basics, stock up at QuickSpice (www.quickspice.com).

berries and other produce: I love the idea of getting all my produce from friends' gardens or farmers' markets. But when that's not practical, look for Driscoll's berries in your supermarket. They're consistently yummy and reliable. For organic and other hard-to-find produce, check out Melissa's (www.melissas.com). I've visited their state-of-the-art operation in Los Angeles and very much like their products.

bacon: It isn't a chapter in *InterCourses*, but it should be. For a fabulously fun selection of bacon, check out The Grateful Palate (www.gratefulpalate.com). I love love love their stuff, and my boyfriend knows it's gonna be a good night when I call to tell him the next installation of my bacon-of-the-month club has arrived.

chocolate: In the 10 years since we first wrote *InterCourses*, chocolate has gone through a transformation extraordinaire. Back then, chocolate meant Hershey's. Dark chocolate contained 45 percent cacao on a good day. And we thought we were living high on the hog when we splurged for a box of Godiva for Valentine's.

Today, chocolate has exploded with new artisan chocolatiers entering the market all the time and well-respected chocolates finding space on standard grocery store shelves. The story of chocolate is a complicated and interesting one. I highly recommend *Chocolate* by Mort Rosenblum to gain a better understanding of the history of chocolate and where it's headed. Until then, just eat. Try. Nibble. Taste. Melt. Drink. There are so many reputable brands, each with so many variations, from single estate bars of criollo cacao to chile-spiked chocolates and couture cocoas. Every time I see a new bar I haven't tried, I pick it up for a home tasting with my boyfriend. It makes us happy, and here's betting it'll do the same for you.

some good chocolate brands:
Amedei (www.amedei-us.com)
Dagoba Organic Chocolate (www.dagobachocolate.com)
E. Guittard (www.eguittard.com)
El Rey (www.chocolates-elrey.com)

Michel Cluizel (www.chocolatmichelcluizel-na.com)
Scharffen Berger (www.scharffenberger.com)
Valrhona (www.valrhona.com)

some talented and/or fun fondeurs in the US:
Chocolate Bar (www.chocolatebarnyc.com)
Fran's (www.franschocolates.com)
L.A. Burdick (www.burdickchocolate.com)
La Maison du Chocolat (www.lamaisonduchocolat.com)
Recchiuti Confections (www.recchiuti.com)
Vosges (www.vosgeschocolate.com)

essential oils: Both Imani Natural Products (www.imaninatural.com) and Laboratory of Flowers (www.labofflowers.com) offer high-quality, reputable oils.

middle eastern ingredients: Ethnic Grocer (www.ethnicgrocer.com) describes itself as a "world market" and offers a wide selection of foods from numerous countries.

spanish ingredients: Manchego cheese and Marcona almonds are both available at my grocery store in Waco, TX, so I'm betting they're available at your supermarket, too. If not, visit LaTienda (www.tienda.com) for a full assortment of Spanish ingredients.

spices, dried herbs, and scented waters: After six months, spices and dried herbs begin to lose their potency. For high-quality spices that will still be packed with flavor when you receive them, stock your pantry from Penzeys Spices (www.penzeys.com) or Vanns Spices (www.vannsspices.com). The Spice House (www.thespicehouse.com) carries rose water and orange blossom water, as well.

olive oils, vinegars, breads, cheeses, honeys, and other condiments: While there are loads of wonderful specialty shops everywhere, Zingerman's has the distinct advantage of having written the book on the best of the best in *Zingerman's Guide to Good Eating*. It's fun to read about the particulars of Serrano ham, lehua blossom honey, and really wild rice, plus they stock loads of fabulous products in their delicatessen that you can buy online. (www.zingermans.com)

massage oils

You can create your own love potion of edible massage oils, bath oils, and salt scrubs with minimal effort, but big results. All you need is a good carrier oil for the base, some high-quality essential oils, and salt. Essential oils are available at many health food and natural food stores. (See page 198 for food-grade suppliers.) Vegetable oils work nicely as the carrier oil – try sweet almond, avocado, olive, sunflower, hazelnut, or jojoba. Mix with your signature concoction of essential oils. Store in an airtight container in a cool, dark place.

basic edible massage oil

1   ounce (2 tablespoons) high-quality carrier oil, such as cold-pressed grapeseed or jojoba oil

6 to 8 drops food-grade essential oil

basic bath salts

2   cups Epsom salt

1   ounce (2 tablespoons) carrier oil, such as grapeseed, sweet almond, or jojoba oil

35 drops essential oil, or combination of essential oils

Pour the carrier oil in a mixing bowl. Add the essential oil combination of your choice, and stir to combine. Add the salt, and stir well to distribute the oil evenly. Place in an airtight jar and let rest a day or two. Shake well before using. Add ½ to 1 cup salt to a hot bath, stirring to dissolve in the water.

basic salt scrub

1½ cups Epsom salt

1½ cups sea salt

1   cup carrier oil, such as grapeseed, sweet almond, or jojoba oil, plus more to cover

Up to 35 drops essential oil, or combination of oils

Combine the salts and place in a lidded jar large enough so that the salt comes only halfway up the jar. Pour the oil into a mixing bowl and stir in the essential oil. Stir in the salt. Return the mixture to the jar and pour in enough oil to just cover the salt.

Brian Skinness with Imani Natural Products shared some of his favorite creations here, and there are hundreds more "recipes" all over the internet. Use these straight as a massage oil or combine with bath water for a sensuously cleansing experience. As with everything else, these recipes work best when altered to your tastes, preferences, fantasies, and creativity. You may also find other recipes throughout the book that work as well on the body as they do on the plate. Have fun investigating.

yummy yummy juicy warm

1   ounce (2 tablespoons) jojoba

21 drops (about 1 dropper full) sandalwood

6   drops ylang-ylang

5   drops steam-distilled lime

the cerebral oil of good feeling

1   ounce (2 tablespoons) jojoba

13 drops frankincense

6   drops patchouli

5   drops steam-distilled lime

relieve anxiety, restore balance

1   ounce (2 tablespoons) jojoba

6   drops geranium

6   drops clary sage

6   drops ylang-ylang

sultry-sweet, aphrodisiac oil

1   ounce (2 tablespoons) jojoba

3   drops jasmine

34 drops sandalwood

aphrodisiac usage guide

winter — The season of frozen noses and warm hearts.
- mexican hot chocolate (page 13)
- cozy vegetable korma (page 42)
- braised beef short ribs with black mission figs (page 196)
- black bean chili (page 109)
- rosemary-bacon croquettes (page 130)

spring — Light and breezy, with the first hints of green.
- steamed asparagus with coco's homemade mayonnaise (page 28)
- pasta with grapes (page 71)
- champagne terrine (page 180)
- springtime salad of pine nuts and avocados (page 169)
- flank steak with rosemary chimichurri (page 140)

aquarius
unpretentious
unusual flavor fusions

sausage
with fig sauce
(page 194)

pisces
exotic
chewy textures and fish

curried oysters
with chardonnay
(page 118)

aries
wide variety
spicy curries and chiles

come-to-jamaica
wings
(page 36)

taurus
indulgent
rich, savory dishes

grilled lamb
with coffee rub
(page 46)

gemini
experimental
tapas-style variety

artichoke bottoms
with chèvre and thyme
(page 93)

cancer
nurturing
traditional comfort food

grand marnier
strawberries over count
biscuits (page 81)

JANUARY　　FEBRUARY　　MARCH　　APRIL　　MAY　　JUNE

aphrodisiacs by the hour: a guide to an InterCourse for any hour of the day

10:00 A.M.	NOON	3:30 P.M.	8:00 P.M.	10:28 P.M.	AFTER MIDNIGHT
lazy morning brunch	simple, but good	afternoon delight	dinner together, from comfy to elegant	before the monologue	late-night adventures (for eating or otherwise)
french toast baked in honey-pecan sauce (page 87)	ham sandwiches on rosemary-manchego scones (page 134)	paws up icy basil lemonade (page 60)	black bean shepherd's pie with corn pudding (page 114)	frozen coffee–almond dessert (page 49)	mascarpone clouds (page 46)
easy strawberry empanadas (page 74)	crab quesadillas with ripe peach salsa (page 157)	strawberries drenched in honeyed cream (page 80)	lemony kefta with israeli couscous (page 145)	toasted nutella and banana sandwiches (page 17)	cabernet sauvignon ice (page 70)
grilled grapefruit with ginger-mint syrup (page 100)	mango-black bean empanadas (page 113)	floral wontons (page 144)	rabbit in mustard sauce (page 138)	honey ice cream with ginger-spiced pecans (page 103)	goldfinger (page 187)
chocolate-stuffed crescent rolls (page 12)	fried oyster salad with rémoulade dressing (page 124)	creamy stuffed figs (page 191)	honeyed duck breast with dried cherries (page 89)	chocolate almond truffles (page 15)	indoor s'mores for grown-ups (page 18)
savory french toast with asparagus and gruyère (page 31)	avocado boats with baby shrimp and ginger sauce (page 105)	shortbread dotted with pine nuts (page 171)	grilled scallops with basil and lavender essence (page 54)	chocolate-dipped meringues with espresso cream (page 50)	jamaican fruit salsa (page 184)
		iced coffee "43" (page 186)			

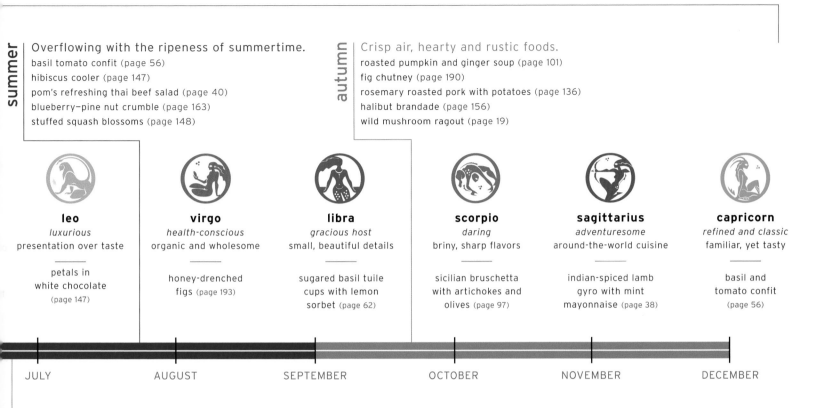

summer

Overflowing with the ripeness of summertime.

basil tomato confit (page 56)
hibiscus cooler (page 147)
pom's refreshing thai beef salad (page 40)
blueberry–pine nut crumble (page 163)
stuffed squash blossoms (page 148)

autumn

Crisp air, hearty and rustic foods.

roasted pumpkin and ginger soup (page 101)
fig chutney (page 190)
rosemary roasted pork with potatoes (page 136)
halibut brandade (page 156)
wild mushroom ragout (page 19)

leo
luxurious
presentation over taste

petals in
white chocolate
(page 147)

virgo
health-conscious
organic and wholesome

honey-drenched
figs (page 193)

libra
gracious host
small, beautiful details

sugared basil tuile
cups with lemon
sorbet (page 62)

scorpio
daring
briny, sharp flavors

sicilian bruschetta
with artichokes and
olives (page 97)

sagittarius
adventuresome
around-the-world cuisine

indian-spiced lamb
gyro with mint
mayonnaise (page 38)

capricorn
refined and classic
familiar, yet tasty

basil and
tomato confit
(page 56)

JULY   AUGUST   SEPTEMBER   OCTOBER   NOVEMBER   DECEMBER

stages of the relationship

flirtation: whetting the appetite – *reeling them in*

steamed artichoke leaves with green goddess dressing (page 96)
done properly, the provocative production of licking, scraping, and
sucking these leaves should turn on any targeted subject

anticipation: checking out the menu – *first date seduction*

honey-glazed salmon (page 154)
makes you look like you can cook, even if you can't

copulation: a dish to remember – *it finally happens*

orange-blossom panna cotta (page 149)
this creamy, jiggly custard is ungodly good and may actually
be incorporated into the event, if so desired

duration: the all-you-can-eat buffet – *aka, the bunny stage*

paws up icy basil lemonade (page 60)
stay hydrated for your marathon events

exploration: tired of leftovers – *needing something new*

malpeque oysters with thai chile mignonette (page 122)
not convinced? read our field test results for this recipe

reconciliation: eating crow – *after an argument*

bittersweet (page 185)
best consumed after angry make-up sex; it'll slow you down after the
frenzy of fighting and reconciling

institutionalization: it's official – *you're mine*

chipotle mac (page 41)
just like you, now that you've got him – sweat pants, no make up,
and a camo thong – it's comfort food with a hidden kick of spice

maturation: like a fine wine – *together forever*

the little death by chocolate (page 183)
anyone together this long deserves something that tastes this good

works consulted

Ackerman, Diane. *A Natural History of Love*. New York: Random House, 1995.

Addison, Josephine and Diana Winkfield. *Love Potions: A Book of Charms and Omens*. Topsfield, MA: Salem House Publishers, 1987.

Aikens, Althea. "Tasty Delights." *Essence* March 2006: 114.

Augarde, Tony, ed. *The Oxford Dictionary of Modern Quotations*. New York: Oxford University Press, 1991.

Bartlett, John and Emily Morison Beck, ed. *Familiar Quotations: A Collection of Passages, Phrases and Proverbs Traced to Their Sources in Ancient and Modern Literature*. Boston: Little, Brown, and Company, 1980.

Bechtel, Stefan. *The Practical Encyclopedia of Sex and Health*. Emmaus, PA: Rodale Press, Inc., 1993.

Bernstein, Sondra. *The Girl & the Fig Cookbook: More Than 100 Recipes From the Acclaimed California Wine Country Restaurant*. New York: Simon & Schuster, 2004.

Brody, Jane E. "Personal Health: A New Look at an Old Quest for Sexual Stimulants." New York Times 4 August 1993: C12.

Carper, Jean. *The Food Pharmacy: Dramatic New Evidence That Food is Your Best Medicine*. New York: Bantam Books, 1991.

Collins, Richard E. "The Cooking Cardiologist." *Total Health* August/September 1998: 41.

Cook, Adrienne. "Plant Herbs; See Your Love Life Grow." *Commercial Appeal* 18 February 1996: F5.

Crenshaw, Theresa L., M.D. *The Alchemy of Love and Lust: Discovering Our Sex Hormones and How They Determine Who We Love, When We Love, and How Often*. New York: G.P. Putnam's Son's, 1996.

Crumpacker, Bunny. *The Sex Life of Food*. New York: St. Martin's Press, 2006.

Fischer, Lynn. *The Better Sex Diet: The Medically-Based Low Fat Eating Plan For Increased Sexual Vitality – In Just 6 Weeks*. Washington, DC: Living Planet Press, 1996.

Fox, Marisa. "Sex Chemicals: Why Pumpkin Pie and Lavender Cause Penile Engorgement and Chocolate is Forbidden in Convents." *Bazaar* February 1996: 92-94.

Harrar, Sari, and Sara Altshul O'Donnell. *The Woman's Book of Healing Herbs: Healing Teas, Tonics, Supplements, and Formulas*. Emmaus, PA: Rodale Press, Inc., 1999.

Hazen, Janet. *Basil*. San Francisco: Chronicle Books, 1993.

Heller, Linda. "Your Health: Alcohol is an Aphrodisiac." *Redbook* October 1994: 33.

Herbst, Sharon Tyler. *The New Food Lover's Companion: Comprehensive Definitions of Over 4000 Food, Wine, and Culinary Terms*. New York: Barron's Educational Series, Inc., 2001.

"Housecalls." *Health Magazine* May/June 1995: 128.

Hyden, Monalisa. "Aphrodisiacs: You Can Do Without Viagra." *Peaceteambook* May 5, 2006: www.peaceteambook.org.

Keith, Lindsey. "Fueling Your Desire?" *The Kentucky Kernel* November 21, 2003: www.kykernel.com.

Lee, Vera. *Secrets of Venus: A Lover's Guide to Charms, Potions, and Aphrodisiacs.* Boston, MA: Mt. Ivy Press, Inc., 1996.

MacClancy, Jeremy. "Food for Love." *Forbes FYI* March 14, 1994: 133+.

Medrich, Alice. *Bittersweet: Recipes and Tales From a Life in Chocolate.* New York: Artisan Publishers, 2003.

Meyer, Clarence. *Herbal Aphrodisiacs From World Sources.* Glenwood, IL: Meyerbooks, Publisher, 1993.

Nickell, Nancy L. *Nature's Aphrodisiacs.* Freedom, CA: The Crossing Press, 2001.

Nordenberg, Tamar. "Looking for a Libido Lift? The Facts About Aphrodisiacs." *FDA Consumer Magazine* January/February 1996: www.fda.gov.

Rosenblum, Mort. *Chocolate: A Bittersweet Tale of Dark and Light.* New York: North Point Press, 2005.

Rosenfeld, Isadore. *Doctor, What Should I Eat? Nutrition Prescriptions for Ailments in Which Diet Can Really Make a Difference.* New York: Random House, 1995.

Smyth, Anna. "Fancy an Aphrodisiac?" *The Scotsman* February 14, 2006: 15.

Sweet, Judith. "Romantic Repast." *The Mercury* February 8, 2006: 33.

Swerdlow, Joel. *Nature's Medicine: Plants That Heal.* Washington, DC: National Geographic Society, 2000.

Warner, Jennifer. "Aphrodisiacs Make Better Flirts and Lovers." Office of Health Education University of Pennsylvania January 26, 2004: www.vpulupenn.edu.

Watson, Cynthia Mervis. *Love Potions: A Guide to Aphrodisiacs and Sexual Pleasures.* New York: G.P. Putnam's Sons, 1993.

Wedeck, Harry E. *A Dictionary of Aphrodisiacs.* New York: M. Evans & Company, Inc., 1992.

Wegner, Fritz, and Emma Curzon. *Heaven on Earth: An Astrological Entertainment with Slides, Wheels, and Changing Pictures.* Boston, MA: Little, Brown, and Company, 1992.

Weinzweig, Ari. *Zingerman's Guide to Good Eating.* New York: Houghton Mifflin Company, 2003.

"What to Eat to Prevent Wrinkles." *Natural Health* April 2002: 26.

Yeager, Selene. *New Foods for Healing: Capture the Powerful Cures of More Than 100 Common Foods.* Emmaus, PA: Rodale Press, Inc., 1998.

index